START FENCING

START FENCING

PROFESSOR A. T. SIMMONDS & E. D. MORTON

• THE •
SPORTSMAN'S
PRESS
LONDON

Published by The Sportsman's Press, 1989

British Library Cataloguing in Publication Data
Simmonds, A. T.
Start fencing.
1. Sports. Fencing – Manuals
I. Title   II. Morton, E. D., 1923–
796.8'6

ISBN 0–948253–40–1

Photoset and printed in Great Britain by
Redwood Burn Limited, Trowbridge, Wiltshire

CONTENTS

CONTENTS

LIST OF ILLUSTRATIONS

FOREWORD

Certain considerations uppermost in our minds prompted us to write this book. The first was that although in terms of analysis and technique Crosnier's *Fencing with the Foil* is still the definitive authority, forty years have elapsed since its publication and the style and tactics of modern fencing have greatly altered. Moreover, fencers today are generally unwilling to practise with the dedication of days gone by, with the result that much modern competitive play is deplorably crude and scrappy.

While we accept that the classical blade actions and elaborate compound attacks which once delighted the connoisseur are no longer applicable, we have attempted to devise a scheme based on classical theory which may still be adapted with success to contemporary conditions. Some such blend, we hold, is essential if any of the artistry of foil play, to say nothing of its pleasure, is to be salvaged for future generations.

This book, which could be of assistance to anyone starting fencing, is aimed primarily at those between eleven and eighteen. Simplicity, therefore, has been our watchword and hence we have not always adhered precisely to Crosnier's analysis of certain actions, especially those in the earlier stages, and we have made no attempt to include the more advanced possibilities, such as *prises-de-fer* and counter-time.

It will be noted that although very few competitions are now fenced with the non-electric foil, we have devoted considerable space to the duties and decisions of the old-fashioned jury, having found by experience that such practice is an excellent way of acquainting those taking part with the rules and conventions of fencing. Despite strongly expressed views to the contrary, to this opinion we adhere, suggesting that the responsibility for training in this branch of fencing lies on the coach.

Our sincere thanks are due to the Amateur Fencing Association for their kind permission to reproduce their diagram of the *piste*; to the Leon Paul Equipment Co., Ltd, for the illustrations of foil handles from their catalogue and for the cover illustration; to Faber and Faber Ltd, for the drawings of grip and target from Crosnier's *Fencing with the Foil*; and to the fencers of Bromley, Cobham Hall, Gravesham, London Hospital and P. J.'s Fencing Clubs, who appear in the photographs, many taken by Howard Ford. Lastly, Mrs R. Puliston, who maintained her traditionally high standard of typing, a joy to authors, publishers and printers alike.

A.T.S.
E.D.M.

1

INTRODUCTION

A SHORT HISTORY OF FENCING

Fencing as we know it really started from about 1450 onwards, when the heavy, straight, two-edged sword of the Middle Ages was replaced by the long, sharp, thin rapier. This was a deadly thrusting weapon. Its length allowed for what was probably the most significant development in fencing – the lunge, as devised by Capo Ferro and Giganti, two great early Italian masters. Its superiority over the 'pass',* the previous method of closing the distance for an attack, was immeasurable and it is astonishing that well over a century elapsed before the 'pass' was finally abandoned as an alternative. The early rapiers were so long that it was impossible to parry with them and for defence (after a brief flirtation by the Italians with a small, round buckler) a dagger, the *main-gauche*, was used in the left hand. Sometimes a cloak was wound round the left hand and arm instead. Other alternatives were pepper, sand or gravel to fling in the opponent's eyes, or a dark lantern whose beam suddenly dazzled him. These last, it must be understood, were devices employed in brawls or ambushes rather than in regular duels or the formal practice of the fencing schools.

As time went on, the rapier was progressively shortened and lightened, so that it was possible to discard the *main-gauche* (dagger). For the first half of the seventeenth century it was still customary to combine defence with attack with the stroke known as the 'time-hit', i.e., a thrust delivered into the opponent's thrust, simultaneously deflecting the latter. The later seventeenth century saw the triumph of the classical French school

* The 'pass' merely consisted in moving the rear leg in front of the leading leg, like taking a step when walking.

over those of Italy and Spain. Its theory and terminology are essentially those of modern foil play. Finally, there appeared the small-sword, the light, stylish, dainty weapon worn by gentlemen of the eighteenth century, perfectly adapted for both attack and defence.

At about the same time, the foil, more or less as we know it, made its appearance as the practice weapon for the small-sword. Until then, actual weapons, with blunted edges and points, or possibly some sort of protection on the latter, had been used for practice or amusement.

Despite numerous edicts by almost every European monarch against duelling, the custom flourished, especially in France in the sixteenth, seventeenth and eighteenth centuries. Henry IV, in the first decade of the seventeenth century, repeatedly banned it; but a swashbuckler himself, with a strong taste for sword-play, he exempted offenders from the very penalties he was committed to enforce and was said to have issued no less than seven thousand pardons. Cardinal Richelieu, the great minister of Louis XIII, was more successful in his merciless attempts to suppress the practice altogether; but Louis XIV reverted to the attitude of his grandfather, condemning duelling at one moment and turning a blind eye to it the next.

The French Revolution and the consequent decline in gentlemanly feeling resulted in the pistol supplanting the sword in most duels during the first half of the nineteenth century. Then, in the second half of that century, the two other weapons used in modern fencing made their appearance. One was the *épée*, a heavier and thicker version of the foil, a thrusting weapon only. This weapon was used both for fencing and, without a button on the point, for actual duels, in which the President and seconds generally made sure that the sword-arm was the target and fatalities were thereby largely avoided.

Simultaneously, there was a most interesting development. The heavy, curved cavalry sabre had long been used in the schools; the Italians now produced a light fencing sabre, retaining only the slightest of curves and well adapted for fast and spectacular exchanges under rules very similar to those of foil. The most recent variety is perfectly straight, but like its prototypes, essentially an edged weapon whose point may also be used.

About 1930 the electrified *épée* and the machine for automatically registering hits were brought into use. Some thirty years later came the electric foil. The sabre has only recently been electrified.

Practically everyone starts with the foil, so the other two weapons are not likely to concern the beginner, though, of course, those of you reading this may like to specialise in one or both later on.

THE ELECTRIC FOIL

The *épée* having been electrified in the 1930s, it was only a matter of time before the same development occurred at foil. The electric foil is heavier than the non-electric weapon; apart from this, the only significant differences are the spring-loaded head and the socket inside the guard into which the body-wire is plugged.

The first occasion of importance in which the electric foil was used was at the World Championships in Rome in 1955. The immediate effect was the sheer devastation of the academic foil-play of tradition – stylish, light and complex – which had not materially altered since the introduction of the wire mask in the late eighteenth century. The early electric foils were heavy, ram-rod-stiff and ill-balanced, thus rendering many of the more subtle blade actions, especially compound attacks, almost impossible to perform. As if this were not enough, it so chanced that the innovation coincided with the appearance, on the international scene, of the eastern Europeans, who, well aware that they could not hope to match the western experts in blade technique, relied rather on extreme fitness, athleticism and opportunism. Such qualities were well suited to bouts judged by the electric apparatus and fought by fencers less concerned with theoretical 'priorities' than making the machine record a hit. Phrases became much shorter and more confused; close-quarter fighting was commonplace; and what might politely be termed *redoublements*, but which were really a succession of frantic jabs at point-blank range, were the order of the day. With the refinement and improvement of the electric weapon, some ground was regained; but much of the old elegance and purity seems gone for ever.

The electric foil is now used at virtually all matches and competitions, even at the most junior level; but there are not lacking those whose opinion commands respect, who argue that there is a strong case for reintroducing the non-electric foil as a separate weapon, with its own matches and competitions, for those who wish to cultivate and preserve some of the skills of a bygone era.

HOW DO I START?

It may be that there is a fencing club at your school, college, youth organisation, or university, in which case there is no problem. If not, ask at your local council offices. Certain local authorities run a fencing club as part of their evening classes. There may be a local Sports Council. Alternatively, ring or write to the:

Amateur Fencing Association
The de Beaumont Centre
83 Perham Road
West Kensington
London W.14   Tel: 01–385 7442

They will be only too glad to let you have a list of all the fencing clubs in your area.

The subscription for clubs being run as evening classes is usually only a few pounds a year for young fencers; in other clubs it may well be more.

You will want to know how much the equipment costs. The answer is, in the very early stage, practically nothing. For the first few sessions, you will need only a tracksuit, or sports shirt and slacks, plus some sort of soft sports or training shoes. Most clubs provide the basic gear, foils, masks, and jackets, for their beginners.

Later on you will almost certainly want your own foil and probably your own mask, jacket and glove. Older fencers who take things seriously have a bag large enough to take a complete set of everything, including the electric over-jacket, the under-plastron, and a number of spare blades to guard against break-ages. This will add up to a large sum of money, but remember, not everything has to be bought at once and the cost can be spread over a number of years. Also, most clubs provide the electric overjackets and in addition there are many senior fencers who are prepared to lend equipment or to sell at a reduced price what they no longer require.

SAFETY

Before going any further, there are several things that must be remembered. The foil, even with its button, or blunt head, can be a killer. So

ALWAYS: 1 Carry your foil with the point downwards.

2 Use full equipment, jacket, glove and above all **MASK**, even for the gentlest warm-up.

NEVER: 1 Use equipment which shows signs of wear, such as a tattered jacket, a rusty mask or a blade which is rusty, out of shape or without a button.

2 At any time fence, or even practice with the weapons, unless the coach or some other official person is present.

2

THE BASICS

The foil   There are two sorts of foil in use, the electric and the non-electric types. The electric foil is now used in practically all matches and competitions. However, you will invariably start with the non-electric weapon. It is lighter and less expensive.

Each part of the foil has its own name. Starting from the point of the non-electric variety, there is the red plastic *button*. The blade, in theory, has two parts: the narrow part nearest the point is called the *foible* (weak part); from about the centre, where it begins to broaden out, is the *forte*, or strong part.

The *hilt* includes all the other 'bits and pieces'. These are the *guard*, the saucer-shaped protection for the hand; inside it, a circular piece of leather, the *cushion*; the handle itself, and at the top of that a heavy metal cap called the *pommel* which helps to balance the weapon. When it is unscrewed, a thin, sharp extension of the blade can be seen, passing up through the handle: this is the *tang* of the blade. Slotting onto the top of the tang is a small screw, the *universal screw*, over which the pommel fits; this screw easily rolls away and is lost, so be careful when undoing it.

On a non-electric foil, there is a leather strap on the handle. It is called the *martingale* and loops over the fingers of the sword-hand, so that the weapon does not fly all over the place to the danger of the bystanders. It is compulsory in a competition.

The electric foil has a spring-head shaped like a very small cylinder instead of a button. An electric wire runs up the blade to a socket inside the guard, into which is plugged the fencer's body wire, connected in turn to the recording apparatus. It has no martingale, as the body-wire serves the same purpose. Its blade is slightly stiffer than that of the older weapon, but otherwise there is little difference and the parts all have the same names.

The Grip   There are two sorts of grip or handle: one is called the

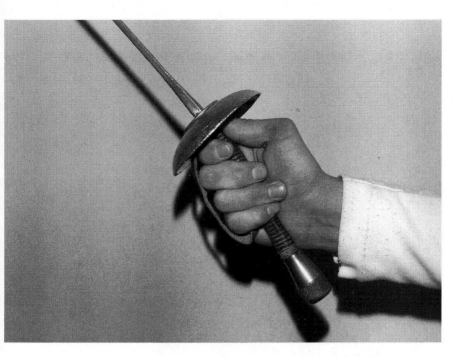

Plate 1
(*above*) Incorrect grip – the 'battleaxe'.
(*below*) 'On guard'.

(*left*) Position and parry of *sixte*.

Plate 2

(*right*) Position and parry of *quarte*.

(*left*) Position and parry of *septime*.

Plate 3

(*right*) Position and parry of *octave*.

Plate 4
(*above*) A hit with a lunge.
(*below*) A lunge – what the defender sees!

'orthopaedic' grip and has all sorts of knobs, bars and curves, the idea being that the hand and fingers close naturally round them and are fixed in one place. You will certainly start with the other sort, called a 'French' grip.

The correct foil grip

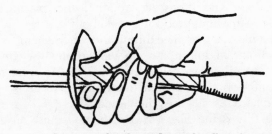

Incorrect: thumb not flat on handle

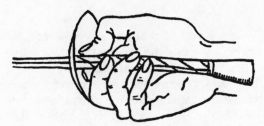

Incorrect: tips of first and second fingers used

Figure 1: The Foil Grip

You will find that it has two broad and two narrow sides and also a slight curve. To hold the weapon properly, the broad side with the curve fitting *into* your hand must be on top. Then the centre section of your first finger is placed underneath the handle as near the guard as it will go. The top section is then hooked round onto the free surface of the handle.

So far, so good. Now the thumb goes *flat* along the top of the handle, with the pommel well into the wrist. The pommel should be in line with the forearm. When you have got this far, you can start to think about the other fingers – numbers two, three and four. They close, not too tightly, on the free surface of the handle, next to the forefinger. Notice they do *not* go on top. In fact, they cannot, if your thumb is where it should be.

The martingale has been mentioned. Your second, third and fourth fingers should be passed through it when placing them on the handle. After that, you can forget about it.

Now about the names. The thumb and forefinger are called the *manipulators* and in due course you will see why; they do most of the work. The others are called the *aids*. The grip of the manipulators should be pretty firm, that of the aids less so. It is a mistake to grip too hard, as this tires the hand.

Perhaps this is the place to explain that there are foils for left-handers, with the blade and handle set properly for them, that is, upside down. Make sure you are using one, if this is what you need.

The salute Before you start fencing, you always salute your opposite number, whoever he or she is – your partner in class-work, your coach when giving you a lesson, your opponent in a bout, whether it is for practice or a proper match. In days gone by, an immensely complicated salute was the fashion, but now it is much simpler. Stand with your heels together, feet at right-angles, mask in your free hand, facing the other fencer. Your foil is held with the point just off the ground and just to the right of the front foot. Raise the sword so that it points straight upwards with the guard on a level with your mouth. Smartly return the weapon to its original position, put on your mask and you are set to go.

In an official match or competition you must salute the President before your opponent.

At the end of the bout, practice, or lesson, another salute is traditional. You will be on guard to start with. Bring the front foot back to touch the rear foot. At the same time, stand upright. As you do so, raise the foil straight above your head and slightly to your right. The arm must not be bent. During all this time, the free arm is lowered to the side.

That gets rid of the complicated part. The last two moves are easy. You bring the weapon down, point still uppermost, with the guard level with your mouth. Then smartly lower the weapon to your right. This was in fact where it started at the very beginning. Finally, shake hands with your opponent with the unarmed hand.

All this may seem a nuisance, but don't forget it. Fencing is a dignified, courteous sport.

On guard   The quick learner is ready to come on guard. This is the starting position. You should then be able to do anything successfully – step forward or back, attack or defend. First, place your heels together with the feet at right angles, the front foot pointing straight ahead, the rear foot pointing to the side. (This is the same as in the salute.) Then take a walking pace forward with the front foot, so that both feet are now more or less under the shoulders. Then bend both knees. They, too, should be at right-angles, one over each foot. Try not to let the rear knee bend forward too much.

This is only half the story. There are still the arms to deal with. First, the sword-arm. Place it on the right-hand side of the body (left, of course, for a left-hander), under the shoulder but not level with it. The hand should be about breast-high and the thumb on top if you are carrying the foil. The elbow is bent, but does not touch the ribs. Instead, it should be several inches clear.

The other arm is held in a raised position slightly behind you. The elbow is level with the shoulder, the forearm more or less vertical and the hand is relaxed and drooping forward.

Now, what about the body? It should not be altogether facing the front, or altogether turned sideways, but about half-way between the two. Watch that front knee at this stage! It should be pointing forwards. Don't lean forward or back. Your body ought to be upright, and you should have an equal amount of weight on both feet.

Throughout the rest of this book, remember that examples apply to right-handed fencers and left-handers should reverse the instructions.

Footwork You are now in a position to practise stepping forward and back. And it is a step, smooth and regular, not a shuffle, nor a hop, skip and a jump. Going forward, the front foot leads. The rear foot follows, covering the same distance. The basic step is not more than about twelve to fifteen inches. Don't be flat-footed and don't stamp. Raise the toes so that the leading foot comes down heel first. Try to do it naturally, as if walking.

When stepping back, it is most important to remember that the rear foot is now the foot to move first and the front foot follows it. Keep practising, backwards and forwards, two or three steps at a time, quite slowly at first. Then gradually increase the speed and the number of steps. Do it as quickly as possible, keeping as upright and still as you can. Some people work their bodies backwards and forwards like the piston of an old-fashioned steam-engine.

Every so often, stop and check your position. You will probably find that you are standing upright. Keep those knees bent! 'Sit down!' as the coaches say. Are your heels still in line, as they should be? And what about your toes? Those in front should point straight ahead, the others should point to the side, not behind. The knees should be pointing in exactly the same way.

Always check the distance between the feet. Most people tend to close them up so that after half-a-dozen steps they are almost touching. The space between them at the end of a series of steps should be exactly the same as when starting.

By this time you are probably groaning. Your legs are agony, to say nothing of that rear arm which is about to drop off. It's unfortunate, but it is a stage everyone must go through. The more you do, the less you feel it, until in the end you don't notice it at all.

This fencing is a sport for heroes . . .

Fencing lines These have nothing to do with the lines on the floor, marking the *piste*, or fencing strip. Fencing lines correspond to parries, and four such lines or parries are in common use today:

Sixte You will remember that when coming 'on guard', you were told to place your hand under the right shoulder, hand breast-high and elbow away from the body. Make sure the pommel is close to the inside of the wrist. The point of the blade should be in line with the opponent's *left* shoulder (whether he is right or left-handed) and roughly on his eye-level when he too, bends his knees in the correct style.*

Now, if your position is correct, your opponent will be unable to hit you from outside your blade, so long as he is in front of you and not absurdly near. This is the favourite fencing line and the one generally taken at the beginning of practice, a lesson and so on. But you don't have to stick to it. You can have any of the other lines you prefer.

Quarte is on the opposite side to *sixte*. Simply move your hand and blade across to the left. Be careful to keep your hand at the same level, don't drop it.

The point stays at the same height, but should now be in line with your opponent's *right* shoulder. To allow for this, you will have to release the pommel a little from your wrist.

Once again, you should be safe from an attack coming from outside your blade.

These two positions, *sixte* and *quarte*, are known as the 'high lines'. *Septime* and *octave* are known as the low lines.

Septime is one of the two lines or parries safeguarding you from a low attack. All you need to do from *quarte* is to lower the point by bending the wrist down. The point should now be at knee-level, but *the hand must stay breast-high*. Otherwise, you are very open to an attack above.

Octave is the other low position. From *septime*, just move the blade straight across so that it protects your right-hand side, but to be quite safe, make sure that the pommel comes back into the wrist again. The point is still knee-high.

Some things are the same in all the above lines:

1 The hand always stays at the same height.
2 The thumb is always on top.
3 The whole blade moves across, point as well as the part near the guard.

* The left-hander's point in *sixte* should *always* be in line with his opponent's right shoulder.

Remember, when changing from *sixte* to *quarte* or back again, not to stop half-way in a central position, neither one thing nor the other. The same is true of the low lines.

So much for sixth, fourth, seventh and eighth, to give them their English names. What happened to first, second, third and fifth? They existed once and are sometimes used today, but not often, so you need not bother about them for the present.

Absence of blade is when fencing takes place without the blades touching each other. You can have your own hand and blade in any of the four lines.

However, when the blades are in contact, it is called an 'engagement' and complications begin to arise.

Engagements   The blades are in contact, crossed, like the conventional sign for a battle on the historical maps. There you are, your blade in (say) the *quarte* line, just as described earlier. You have even remembered to keep your point in line with your opponent's right shoulder. So you should be safe *if* – and this is the point – *if* your opponent's blade is on the outer or left-hand side of your own blade.

If it is on the inside (your right-hand side) you are fearfully open to a straight thrust – that is, your opponent has only gleefully to extend his arm and hit. The same is true if you are in your marvellously correct *sixte* position. You are only safe if your opponent's blade is once more on the outside, this time the right-hand side, of your own. Otherwise, you will soon be in trouble. Try it with a friend to see. You can do it with your forefingers at any time.

When actually fencing, you will often find that when the blades are engaged, you are both slightly open to a straight thrust. Watch this! You can both be equally at risk!

Covering   What, then, is to be done if, to your horror, you suddenly find yourself in the really risky position described above?

One escape route is called *covering*. Using your own blade, push your opponent's blade across your body, so that it ends up on the *outside* of yours. Make sure that you finish up properly 'covered' and that he cannot hit you with that sudden straightening of the arm.

Change of engagement This is an even better way of protecting yourself, because it makes things rather more difficult for your opponent. We will again suppose you are in *sixte*, but your opponent's blade is on the *inside* of yours. You change your engagement by dropping the point, passing it under your opponent's blade, collecting the latter, and engaging again on the side opposite to where you started. You are still in *sixte*, but if you have done it properly your opponent cannot now hit you with a straight thrust.

There are certain attacks which are something like the change of engagement, because they pass underneath your opponent's blade and hit him on the opposite side. All such actions should be made, as far as possible, with the fingers. Keep your weapon close to your opponent's and avoid great circular, windmill actions with the hand and arm.

The target is the part of the body where you must place your hits if they are going to count. Without going into exact details, it is enough to say that at foil, the target is the trunk, without the arms, legs and mask. In front, there is also the 'V' between the groins. The back and sides are also target areas, as long as they are above the hips.

In theory, the foil target is divided into quarters. Each quarter can be protected from an attack on the *outside* by coming on guard in the line of the same name. When an attack is switched *inside* your blade, then of course you must move it across to meet the attack. But more of that in the section on parries.

The hit Now that you have some idea of coming on guard, engaging and changing the engagement, and what the target is, you can try a hit.

It is best, at the start, not to complicate things too much by crossing swords and worrying about who is covered and who isn't. Let your partner just stand fully facing you, foil lowered. You take a correct on-guard position just far enough away to be able to hit with a full extension of the sword-arm and without any footwork. Check the distance first.

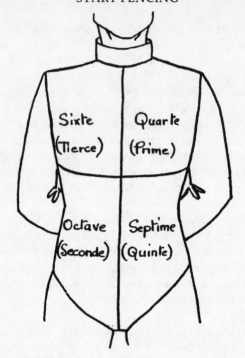

Figure 2: The Target and its Quartering into Lines

Many beginners lean forward to hit, quite unnecessarily, and never really straighten the arm at all. Keep the body as still as possible, with both feet firmly on the ground (no trophies are awarded for an imitation of Eros in Piccadilly). It is the arm alone that is supposed to move, lightly, from the elbow.

Squeeze with the thumb and forefinger as the sword-arm starts to move. At the same moment as the arm is straightened, the hit is made by placing the point on the target. The blade should curve slightly in an upward direction as the hit arrives, but not too much.

These points are worth remembering and listing separately:

1 Don't lean
2 Don't punch
3 Don't move the legs at all

The Lunge Now is the time to try the hit with the lunge. In ninety-nine cases out of a hundred, you will have to lunge if you want to attack and reach your opponent.

The first stage is almost, if not quite, the most important. Whatever else happens, you must extend the sword-arm first. Do it as fast as you like, but lightly. Don't punch from the shoulder as though you were a heavy-weight boxer about to lay his opponent on the canvas. Even this isn't as simple as it sounds. In extending the arm, fencers stand up. That is wrong, because it alters the height of the point. So you might hit off-target or miss altogether.

So, it's probably start again! Straighten that arm and make sure your knees are still bent. Now you can lunge – or can you? The front foot has to be lifted off the floor and put down a long stride ahead. To do this with the right balance, you must lift the toes first and put the foot down again, heel first, and toes last. This is just like the step forward. Make sure that the front foot is pointing straight ahead and the knee is directly over it, neither in front nor behind.

So much for the front leg. The rear foot remains flat on the ground – repeat, flat! – and the rear knee is straightened.

That, unfortunately, isn't all. The rear arm must not be forgotten. As you lunge, it should be lowered behind you so that it finishes just above the rear leg. The palm should be turned *outwards*. All this is not just because it looks pretty (though it does), but because this action of the arm is a great help to the lunge. It helps you to stay on course. Also, if it is lowered smartly, about half-way through the lunge, it pushes you forward those few extra inches which can be vital. What you must avoid doing, is just to let it drop feebly before you lunge at all. That is worse than useless.

You will probably agree that the lunge is more painful than the footwork. Yet if you want to become any sort of a fencer, you must practise it until you feel like howling for mercy. Fencers have been known who made thirty, forty, or fifty lunges each morning or evening in the kitchen with a poker, or in their bedroom with a walking-stick or umbrella. You will be glad to hear that you are not necessarily advised to do exactly the same. It is far better to do half-a-dozen lunges really well, checking your position before a long glass if there is one, than rushing your way through some fantastic number to boast about, flopping about all over the place and only repeating your faults.

A few vital points which can be repeated over and over again:

1 Knee directly over front foot. (Not in front of or behind it.)
2 Front thigh parallel to ground.
3 Chest still half-facing front.
4 Head above right thigh. (Not falling to your left, or in advance of front foot.)
5 Unarmed hand palm outwards.
6 Sword-hand – keep thumb on top!

Recovery to guard Sometimes, for tactical reasons, you will want to remain on the lunge. More often than not, you will recover to the on-guard position if your attack is parried. Anyway, you will have to make the recovery sooner or later, so it is very important to do it in the best possible way.

Avoid anything like a giant heave – slow, clumsy, exhausting. The first and most important move is to bend the rear knee. This shifts the weight from the front to the rear leg, and automatically causes the toes of the leading foot to rise. Then you can push off with the front heel and so bring the front foot, just off the floor, back to its normal on-guard position. At the same time, raise the rear arm to the normal on-guard position. While recovering, the sword-arm should remain straight as a form of protection. The elbow should not be bent into the *quarte* or *sixte* positions until the recovery is otherwise complete.

Make sure that when you have come back on guard, your position is really correct, and in particular, your knees are bent. If all has gone as it should, you will be able to fence on and deal with any riposte or fresh attack from your opponent.

Some people are lazy about the front foot and either drag it back along the ground or only withdraw it half or two-thirds of the full distance. This results in a straddled, badly-balanced position.

The recovery to guard, like the lunge itself, should be as 'flat' as possible. It is wasted effort to go right up in the air and down again in almost exactly the same place.

The fencing measure is the distance between the fencers and is such that when you fully lunge, you can reach and hit your opponent. Of course, you are not able to keep at this exact distance all the time. In modern fencing it is common to stay slightly beyond this distance most of the time, closing in for an attack when the opportunity occurs. Always be very careful if you feel that you are at a distance where your opponent could hit you by extending the arm, without lunging at all. It is true that you might be able to hit him equally well, but it could spell danger for *you*, if you are not on the alert or he has deflected your blade while coming forward. It means that you are within his riposting distance and he is *inside* your fencing measure, and you will find it very difficult to parry effectively.

3

ATTACKS

There are four **Simple Attacks** – the Straight Thrust, the Disengagement, the Cut-over and the Counter-disengagement.

The **straight thrust** is when you extend the sword-arm fully, point in line with the target, attack with a lunge and hit the target.

The **disengagement** starts when the two blades are engaged or touching. Take your blade away from your opponent's, pass it underneath his, straightening the sword-arm as you do so, aim the point at the target and lunge to hit as with the straight thrust. Try to perform the action as much as possible with the fingers, rather than a clumsy arm movement.

The **cut-over** is the one that goes *over* your adversary's blade. Pull your own blade back towards you by bending the elbow; carry it over his point; then extend and lunge. This bending and extension of the sword-arm must be as fast as possible.

The cut-over is generally performed from an engagement. Press slightly on the other's blade as you draw back the elbow and you should hear a satisfactorily dramatic *zipp*.

The **counter-disengagement** is the exception to the rule – you have to wait for your opponent to move first. If the blades are engaged, but he can be hit by your straight thrust, he may try to protect himself by a change of engagement – that is, dropping his blade beneath yours and engaging in the opposite line. By following his blade round in a circle, at the same time straightening your arm with a spiralling action, you are in a position to lunge and hit in the usual way.

Trouble arises from the fact that, according to which side you start from, the direction of the circles is different.

1 If you start in *sixte* and he tries to change the engagement to *quarte*, you must follow him round to your right (clockwise).

2 If starting in *quarte*, go to your left (anti-clockwise).

There must be no blade contact at any stage for a successful counter-disengagement.

Remember to use your fingers as much as possible, rather than your arm.

Try it, but don't worry if it ends in a mess. It will come in time.

Low-line attacks can be by straight thrust or a theoretical disengagement from a high-line position. In either case, extend the sword-arm with a turn of the wrist while doing so. If you are attacking into your (right-handed) opponent's *octave*, this turn must put the sword-hand into pronation (nails underneath). If into his *septime*, supinate (nails on top). This wrist action allows the natural bend of the blade to be turned into the target and ensures a better 'fix'. Also, it avoids the danger of the blade catching on the underside of the opponent's sword-arm and breaking. In either case, make absolutely sure that:

1 The hand is definitely low.
2 The point is slightly higher than the hand, so that it travels upwards to the target.

This somewhat awkward and unnatural position must be maintained while lunging. Therefore, 'lock' the elbow while you do so. Otherwise, you will find your point wavers, you will be aiming downwards, not up, and your hit will arrive off target.

There is a good deal of disagreement among masters about the hand position. They all agree that it must definitely be lowered – it is not just a case of aiming the point downwards. But some say 'supinate' for all low-line attacks, others prefer to keep the thumb on top. Beginners had better do exactly as their coach tells them. Later on, they may be allowed some freedom of choice. Then they will be able to decide which particular method suits them best.

4

DEFENCE

There are three types of parry – **simple, semi-circular** and **circular**. The simple parries are *quarte* and *sixte*, the semi-circular are *septime* and *octave*. The third type are the circular parries of *quarte* and *sixte*.

Parries in general   To parry is to protect yourself against an attack by placing your foil in the way so that the attacking blade is turned aside. Notice we have said 'placing your foil in the way'. You don't beat or slash at your opponent's weapon. You lose control if you do. Instead, you quite quietly put your *forte* against his *foible* – the strong part of the blade of course masters the weak.

The object of any parry is not just to defend yourself, but also to prepare the way for a riposte. Therefore, the movements of the sword must be as small as possible, and the point at all times kept as near as possible to your opponent's target, in line with his shoulder.

Remember, all parry positions are the same as the fencing lines taken when on guard, and *vice versa*.

The **simple parry**   You are on guard with your blade in *sixte*. If properly covered, you can only be hit in *quarte*, on the inside of your blade. So you carry your blade across to your left, to meet that attack, *forte* to *foible*. There are a lot of things that can go wrong and need attention.

1 Keep the hand at the same height.
2 Keep the thumb on top.
3 Let the pommel come slightly out of the wrist so that –
4 The point is in line with your opponent's right shoulder.

It is, in fact, the same as a properly covered position in the *quarte* line.

Alternatively, you are on guard or engaged in *quarte*. Now the attack comes towards your *sixte* side, so you move the blade across to your right. You should finish up in the normal *sixte* position, point straight ahead, properly covered. But to make sure of this, the last fingers (aids) must be closed on the pommel to bring it into the wrist at the moment of contact.

The **semi-circular parry**   Now there are indeed rocks ahead. You are in the high line (*quarte* or *sixte*). Your opponent disengages, but doesn't lift up his point on the other side of your weapon. Instead, he comes in very low. You will find that neither your simple nor circular parries are any help. Your defence is a semi-circular parry finishing in the low line. This means that your point must trace a semi-circle in the air. You go *over* the attacking blade to collect it and you finish with your point low. *But your hand is still breast high.*

Semi-circular parries finish on the same side of your target. *Quarte* ends in *septime*, *sixte* in *octave*. It helps if you know the alphabet! From *quarte* to *septime*, trace the back of the capital D in the air. From *sixte* to *octave* trace the capital C. Remember, it is the point which makes the letter, not your hand or arm. The semi-circular movement is brought about by the wrist. When finishing in *octave*, the elbow should be kept under the shoulder, not stuck out.

The **circular parry** is an alternative to the simple parry. Somebody once called it the 'twiddle' parry. You are in *sixte*. Your opponent comes under your blade to attack (that's the disengagement). Your instinctive or simple parry, as we said earlier, is to take your blade over to *quarte*; but you can as readily protect yourself and infuriate your opponent by dropping your point under his as if starting a disengagement yourself, lifting it on the other side, collecting his blade and parrying him in *sixte*. In other words, your blade has described a circle, clockwise towards your right, and you finish in exactly the same position you started in, but with his blade outside yours. This goes for everything – your hand and elbow should start and finish in the same proper *sixte* position.

If engaged in *quarte*, your opponent must disengage to your right-hand side, into the *sixte* line. The circular parry of *quarte* is anti-clockwise, outwards to your left. The same rules for your hand and arm still hold.

Several points of special importance connected with the circular parry are:

1 Don't lift the hand.
2 Move it as little as possible. Your point, not your hand, makes the circle.
3 Don't pull the arm back towards the body. Parry slightly forward, if anything.
4 And, as for all disengagements, changes of engagement, etc., use the fingers as much as possible.

Don't despair if you have difficulty at first. Much of the trouble arises from the fact that after completing the circle, too many beginners want to add something more onto it and end up with their foils pointing downwards. That is wrong! When starting in *quarte* or *sixte*, the point should be up. After the parry, it should be exactly where it started.

If you seem to be making the circle correctly, but your opponent is still hitting you, it is probably because you are too close.

The counter-attack or stop-hit It has always been said that the best form of defence is attack. While not always entirely true, there is something in it and the same may be said of the counter-attack or stop-hit.

The stop-hit is an attack on your opponent's attack or advance, but as will be explained later, it only counts in certain circumstances. So be wary of using it too much; you will soon see why. But it is very useful against the opponent who steps too close, leaving himself open. You 'stop' his advance by extending your arm and hitting just as he comes within distance. Keep the knees well down, otherwise your hit may go too high. Don't lean forward too much, or you may overbalance.

You can stop-hit by straight thrust or disengagement. If disengaging, don't catch his arm or blade by straightening your arm too early. You can also stop-hit with a lunge, which in some ways is better still, as you may catch him a shade earlier. But however you do it, you must never stop-hit once he has actually begun his attack. That *must* be parried. The reason is that a stop-hit, to be allowed, must arrive one period of fencing time ahead of the attack.

A 'period of fencing time' is the time taken by a fencer to perform any one movement of blade or body.

5

RIPOSTES AND COUNTER-RIPOSTES

Ripostes Your opponent has attacked, you have parried. So now, you are, so to speak, in the driving seat. He could be at your mercy. An attack which you make immediately after your parry is called a *riposte*.

If, after extending the arm, your point is just short, don't *lean*; that way, you overbalance. A slight lunge will be all that is required.

Ripostes, like attacks, can be made in different ways. A riposte can be 'direct', like the straight thrust, staying on the same side of your opponent's blade. Or it can be a disengagement, cut-over, or anything else. To some extent, what your opponent does following your parry of his attack decides the type of your riposte. If he leaves himself open, make the direct riposte as fast as you can.

Many fencers with some experience expect this and parry very quickly, putting their blade where you want yours to go. The answer to that is to riposte by disengagement. As soon as you feel the 'pull' on your weapon, drop your point, pass it beneath his blade, lift it and straighten your arm on the other side. But notice this: you must not straighten your arm until after you have passed underneath the other blade; otherwise you risk catching your own blade on some part of your opponent's weapon or sword-arm.

While disengaging, try to keep your hand and sword-arm as still as possible. The more you wave them about, the more likely you are to get entangled with some non-target surface of your opponent's body or equipment.

You can riposte by cut-over, if you prefer it to the disengagement.

Ripostes can be simple or compound (i.e., more than one blade action). They may also be immediate or delayed, that is, after holding the opponent's blade.

The **Counter-riposte**   This is spectacular, everyone enjoys doing it, and a satisfactory *tick-tack* sound should result.

Suppose you attack, your opponent parries and ripostes and you are good enough to parry that riposte while on the lunge. Your next attempt to hit him is the counter-riposte.

Like the riposte itself, it corresponds to the attacks you know. It can be direct, by disengagement, by cut-over and so on. Usually, for the sake of speed, it is direct. Nevertheless, you can think about a disengagement or cut-over if you feel the 'pull' on your blade which shows your opponent is expecting the direct counter-riposte.

What happens if he is able to parry your counter-riposte? He then makes what is called the *second* counter-riposte. (Yours, obviously, was the first.) It may help to make things clearer if they are set out in their proper order:

A   attacks
B   parries and ripostes

A   parries and counter-ripostes (the first)
B   parries and counter-ripostes (the second)

Just like ripostes, all counter-ripostes can be simple or compound, immediate or delayed.

6

PREPARATIONS OF ATTACK

As the name suggests, these are actions designed to prepare the way for an attack. They can be made with the blade or by means of footwork. Preparations with the feet are to advance or retire with the object of gaining an advantage in *distance* over your opponent. Preparations with the blade gain *time* on him.

The step forward and **step back** The step forward is the simplest and most obvious form of preparation, to get within lunging distance of your opponent. But you can also step back, to tempt him into following you and perhaps coming a shade too close, when you can take him by surprise.

Preparations with the blade Among these are the *attacks on the blade*, namely:

1 The **beat** and its several variations.
2 The **pressure**.
3 The *froissement*.

1 The **beat**, as is clear from the name, is to give your opponent's blade a sharp tap, so as to displace it and open the way for your attack. Beat your opponent's blade just forward of its centre, where the *forte* is narrowing into the *foible*. You should not beat into his *forte*, because that has no effect.

The beat in *quarte* is a little different from the beat in *sixte*. Coming at the blade as though about to engage in *quarte*, slightly unclose your 'aids', so that the pommel comes away from your wrist. Then smartly close them to make the blade give a sharp tap against your opponent's. The beat is not a savage slash, as though chopping wood, or like a comic-strip schoolmaster bringing his cane forcibly down on a tight trouser-seat.

In *sixte*, it is very difficult to use the fingers. Therefore, the wrist comes more into use, but the action must be carefully controlled.

Beats are less common in the low lines, but none the less useful. Use the fingers in *septime*, but in *octave* the wrist alone comes into play.

Once the beat has been made, immediately extend the arm and lunge. The rules say that your opponent must parry before he tries anything else, unless you pause and waste time. Provided your attack instantly follows the beat, and he hits you without parrying first, his hit will not count – that is, of course, as long as you do manage to hit him!

The **beat** can be made **downwards** against the opponent whose arm and blade are somewhat lower than they ideally should be. The wrist has to be turned inwards towards the left, so that the beat can be made at an angle of at least forty-five degrees. The blades meet just above their centres. The thumb remains on top and the wrist and fingers are used just as in the ordinary beat in *quarte*. The wrist must then be straightened and the sword-arm extended with point threatening the target before the lunge is made in the normal way.

The **upward beat** is employed against the person who holds his blade rather higher than usual. The wrist is bent inwards, as for the downward beat, but this time the opponent's blade is deflected upward by means of a wrist action only. It is very important not to let the point fly upwards out of line, so keep the wrist movement well under control. Then straighten the wrist and arm and lunge in the usual way.

The **change-beat** is very like the change of engagement. You lower your point under your opponent's, lift it on the other side of his weapon, but instead of engaging, make a beat. Change-beats are generally made from *sixte* into *quarte*, as most fencers beat more sharply and confidently in that line.

The **double-beat** is two beats made quickly on the same side of the blade, one after the other. The arm is not extended between the two.

The **double change-beat** is first one change-beat, then another. The second is therefore made on the same side of your opponent's blade as you started from.

Remember, all beats should be made with a bent arm; but it must be straightened before attacking to ensure 'right of way'.

2 The **pressure** is another useful preparation. Again it is what it sounds like. By means of a wrist action, press your blade against your opponent's, taking it out of line and so making room for your attack. If he presses back, it can be a great opportunity to drop your point beneath his and hit him with a disengagement.

3 The *froissement* is a strong grazing action designed to force the opponent's blade out of line. Using the *forte* of your weapon, bring it sharply down and along his, from his *foible* to about the middle. This is done by a turn of the wrist and a half-way extension of the sword-arm only. The point should be rather higher than the hand. The blade makes an angle of about forty-five degrees with the opponent's.

There is some dispute as to whether the hand should be pronated in both *quarte* and *sixte* or in *quarte* only. One very great master says 'Pronate in both'; but some have found that better results are obtained by supination in *sixte*, when the natural curve of the weapon keeps the point closer to the target.

The *froissement* is not used as often as it could be at electric foil today, due to the present habit of fencing with absence of blade. Few present-day coaches can teach the application of its use under the prevailing conditions.

Beats, pressures and steps are often joined together. As fencers beat, or make a pressure, they can also step forward to gain distance. This is often the reason for a double beat. Two steps are often needed to catch up with an opponent who is evidently in difficulties and trying to get away; so a beat is given with each step, to keep him occupied and stop him suddenly extending his arm, which might be dangerous.

7

RENEWED ATTACKS

There are three ways of renewing the attack, the *remise, redouble-ment* and *reprise*. These should only be executed if your opponent, having parried the attack, fails to riposte. This may be because he is stupid, lacks confidence, or is uncertain what to do next. In all these cases it is quite in order for you to have a 'second go'.

The *remise* If your opponent parries, then takes his blade away and does not riposte, leave your arm quite straight and simply place your point on the part of his target that he has left open. Sometimes it is possible to *remise* even if he continues to hold your blade with his parry. In that case, place the point on target on the same side of his weapon by exerting a certain amount of pressure.

The *redoublement* When the opponent holds your blade with his parry, it is more usual to renew the attack by a *redoublement*. This means that there must be an additional blade action, finishing on the opposite side to the parry. Most commonly, this is done by a disengagement, though a cut-over could be used, and there are other possibilities for more advanced fencers.

The *reprise* This is the odd one out, because it involves the use of the feet as well as the blade. It is needed when your opponent, having parried but not riposted, steps back to get out of harm's way. If so, you can follow him by the action called the *reprise*. And if you thought the lunge was painful, wait till you try this.
   Your sword-arm must remain straight. You then raise the rear arm and bring forward the rear foot so that you are again in the on-guard position. Try not to heave the body forward, but bring up that rear leg by bending the knee. You should end up well-

balanced, with knees bent. Then comes another lunge along with any blade action that threatens the open part of his target.

All through the recovery forward, you should hold your opponent's blade until you are quite ready for the second lunge. If you let it go, you encourage him to stick out his arm and hit you at some stage of your forward movement.

Not only attacks, but ripostes and counter-ripostes can be renewed in the ways just described. The renewal of a riposte, particularly, can be a very paying game. Your opponent, having parried your riposte, may think that the danger is over for the time being and that he can afford to relax. A sudden renewal of the riposte may catch him sleeping.

But be sensible about all this and make sure the conditions are right. Nothing is worse than to see two fencers who have apparently gone mad, jabbing away frantically at each other with seemingly endless renewals, no-one knowing in the end who, if anyone, got the deciding hit. All renewals must arrive on target one movement ahead of any riposte or counter-riposte. So it is really safest, if you are going to renew an attack, to be pretty sure that your opponent seldom or never ripostes, or, at least, is slow in doing so.

8

COMPOUND ATTACKS AND SUCCESSIVE PARRIES

Compound attacks are attacks of more than one blade action.

Sometimes you will find that your opponent is parrying all your simple attacks, such as your straight thrust, disengagement, etc., with confidence and ease. You just cannot beat him for speed; however fast you go, he still parries. The compound attack is the answer.

The most common compound attack is the **one-two**. From an engagement (say in *sixte*) you pass under his blade, straightening your arm and so threatening him with a disengagement. Swallowing the bait, he parries *quarte*, but before he can touch your blade, you disengage again and hit him on the other side of his weapon where he least expects it.

This is not quite as easy as it sounds and needs great skill in the timing. Apart from anything else, you have got to combine the bladework with the lunge. If you can possibly manage it, the lunge should start with the first disengagement, so that the second disengagement is done while your front foot is still in the air. We call this a 'progressive' compound attack. The 'progressive' attack is highly effective because it forces your opponent to parry early, which is what you want. The earlier his parry, the more time and space you have to avoid it.

The *Doublé* is another example of a compound attack. It is a disengagement followed by a counter-disengagement.

Let us suppose that you are in the same position as you were when starting the one-two, that is, engaged in *sixte*. You make a disengagement as before, but this time your opponent, instead of parrying *quarte*, is unkind enough to reply with the circular parry of *sixte*. So you must avoid this different parry, not with an ordinary disengagement, but by following his blade round in a circle, anti-clockwise – in other words, a counter-disengagement.

At this stage, the intelligent reader is going to say: 'All very well –
I make my disengagement, but what then? How do I know what
sort of parry he is going to make?' The answer is, you don't. It is
possible, of course, to disengage from the on-guard position and
wait to see what parry he takes. But this is not recommended, as
he may suddenly attack you as you pause. It is better to rely on
the progressive attack. You have got to be a bit of a mind-reader
and a bit of a fortune-teller and accept that there will be times
when you guess wrong.

Another thing about compound attacks, arising from the
above, which may well have become clear anyway. You can start
with a disengagement, a straight thrust, or a cut-over. But the
second part of your compound attack depends on the parry taken
by your opponent. If it is a simple parry, it can only be deceived
by a disengagement. If it is a circular parry, the answer *must* be a
counter-disengagement.

Remember these three points in connection with any compound attack:

1 The first blade action must look as much like a real attack as
   possible. So as well as making the attack progressive, the
   point of the weapon must very definitely be directed at the
   target, not away at the side.
2 The arm must be straightened on the first blade action.
   (Again, it looks more threatening.)
3 Once straightened, the arm must not be bent during the
   second part of the attack. Any disengagement which
   forms part of a compound attack should be made with the
   fingers as far as possible.

Successive parries are at least two parries taken one after the
other and are the answer to a compound attack.

It is splendid to be hitting your opponent time after time with a
masterly series of compound attacks. It is not so good to be on the
receiving end, so in case your opponent is an expert, you must
know how to use successive parries.

Let us look at the one-two attack again, this time from the
viewpoint of the defender. You are engaged in *sixte* when your
opponent makes what is apparently an attack by disengagement.
Over goes your blade to parry *quarte*, but to your dismay you
meet with nothing but thin air; he has made the second dis-

engagement and there is his blade, homing in now at about a hundred miles an hour into your open *sixte* line. Obviously, you must parry again – the 'successive' parry; the most natural and easy one is a simple parry, back to *sixte*.

Certain points hold good with all successive parries:

1 The parries must be carefully controlled – no slashing, or letting the point fly to one side.
2 The hand must be kept at the same height, always breast-high.
3 When returning to *sixte* from *quarte*, it is more important than ever not to drop the hand or pull the elbow back to the body.

Once you have 'found' your opponent's blade by means of these successive parries, you are of course able to riposte in the normal way.

There are other examples of successive parries which can be used to protect you against the one-two attack described above. Following your first parry of *quarte*, your second can be either the circular parry of *quarte*, or the semi-circular parry of *septime*.

Matters are rather different when it is a case of defending yourself against the *doublé*. In the first place, your opponent can only attack by a *doublé* if your first parry is circular. After that you have a choice of a simple, another circular, or a semi-circular parry to catch up with the second part of his attack. An example is given later in the exercise section, but meanwhile the computer experts can no doubt work out the possibilities.

If the whole thing sounds horribly complicated, don't be put off. You don't have to grasp it all perfectly at once. Try some of the examples given further on, and a good deal of it will probably fall into place when you are actually doing them.

9

EXERCISES

INDIVIDUAL EXERCISES

A few choice forms of torture! To begin with, you should only attempt two or three examples of each and may not even work through the whole list in one session. Gradually increase the number of times you do each exercise, as your fitness increases. Eventually, you should be able to complete ten, fifteen, twenty, or even more repetitions of each exercise, one after the other, without a total collapse.

1 Lunge, place both hands on leading thigh. Lean back, so that weight is on rear foot and rear knee is bent. Front foot remains flat on ground. Then lean forward, pressing hands on thigh, which should be horizontal. Do this repeatedly and rhythmically. Increase the number of times as you get used to it.

2 Five lunges, stopping after each to check position. Make particularly sure that back foot has not been allowed to slide forward.

3 Lunge and stay on the lunge with sword-arm extended. Keeping front heel on floor, raise toes and tap the ground. Try not to lean back too much.

4 Lunge and rock backwards and forwards rhythmically. As you rock back with weight on rear foot, rear knee bends, front toes are lifted, rear arm is raised to on-guard position. Rear arm is lowered as you lunge forward again.

5 As above, but this time front foot is lifted clear of the floor, as you rock backwards. Control your forward action, don't shake the whole building as your front foot comes down.

6 Lunge, recover to guard forwards, by bringing rear foot forward and raising rear arm. Then replace rear foot backwards and lower arm to resume lunge position. Bend rear knee on forward action, keep head well up. Practise rhythmically, but slowly at first. Increase speed later as your fitness improves.

7 Lunge and *reprise*, recover backwards to guard after second lunge.

8 As above, but begin with step forward and finish with step back after final recovery.

EXERCISE IN PAIRS

In all cases, partners should take turns in attacking and defending, changing over after, at most, half-a-dozen repetitions.

Stepping forward and back
1 Both fencers on guard in *sixte*, absence of blade. Lunging distance.
2 Attacker leads by stepping forward or back.
3 Defender does the opposite.
   Vary speed and number of steps taken.
   Stop every now and then, check distance.

Change of engagement
1 Both fencers on guard in *sixte*, blades engaged, lunging distance.
2 Attacker may be slightly uncovered.
3 Attacker changes to *quarte* and makes sure he is properly covered, if necessary with a covering action following the change.
   The change of engagement may be attempted from a *quarte* engagement.
   It may also be made with the attacker's step forward. Defender should step back.

SIMPLE ATTACKS
1 *Straight thrust*
   (*a*) Both fencers on guard in *sixte*, absence of blade.

(b) Attacker extends arm, lunges and hits.

The straight thrust may then be tried from an engagement. The defender must be slightly uncovered, or it will not be possible.

Make sure that after several attempts you have not closed in on each other. If the blades are bending almost double or your sword-hand is much higher than the place where your point arrives on target, you are too near each other.

2 *Disengagement*
  (a) Both fencers on guard in *sixte*, blades engaged.
  (b) Defender must be well covered to allow attacker to disengage and hit on the opposite side of the target.
  (c) Attacker must make certain that his sword-arm is straightened before lunging.

The disengagement may then be attempted from an engagement in *quarte*.

3 *Cut-over*
  (a) Both fencers on guard in *sixte*, blades engaged.
  (b) Defender well covered – same reason as above.
  (c) Attacker should clear opponent's blade by bending his elbow, not by hitting the ceiling with his point.
  (d) As usual, sword-arm must be straightened before lunging.

The cut-over may also be done from a *quarte* engagement.

4 *Counter-disengagement*
Remember, this one is different! The defender must *start* the exercise.
  (a) Both fencers on guard in *quarte*, blades engaged, attacker covered.
  (b) Defender therefore moves first, changing engagement to *sixte*.
  (c) As he does so, attacker follows his blade round in a circle (anti-clockwise) at the same time straightening sword-arm Lunge follows.

Do not let your opponent 'find' your blade as he changes his engagement. You must avoid his attempt to make contact in the new line.

Next, try the counter-disengagement from *sixte* (attacker again covered). This is more difficult because of the need to make your attack over the defender's sword-arm.

5 *Low-line attacks*
    (*a*) Both fencers on guard in *sixte*, absence of blade.
    (*b*) Attacker extends sword-arm downwards, pronating hand if attacking opponent's *octave*, supinating for *septime*. Make sure, by bending wrist, that point is higher than hand.
    (*c*) Extend sword-arm, lunge and hit, keeping elbow rigid.
Ensure blade is angulated into target and point is *above* hand before lunging.

It is as well to pause after stage (*b*) and check hand and blade position before trying the low-line attack as one complete action.

Parries
1 *Simple Parry*
    (*a*) Both fencers on guard in *sixte*, absence of blade.
    (*b*) Attacker lunges with straight thrust.
    (*c*) Defender parries *quarte*.
Then both come on guard in *quarte*. Defender parries *sixte*.

2 *Semi-circular Parry*
    (*a*) Both fencers on guard in *sixte*, blades engaged.
    (*b*) Defender covered.
    (*c*) Attacker lunges with disengagement.
    (*d*) Defender parries *octave*. He should trace a capital 'C' in the air, point going *over* opponent's blade.
Then:
    (*a*) Fencers engaged in *quarte*.
    (*b*) Defender covered.
    (*c*) Attacker lunges with disengagement.
    (*d*) Defender parries *septime*. He should trace the back of a capital D in the air, going *over* the opponent's blade.
With either semi-circular parry, the defender should keep the hand breast-high and as still as possible.

3 *Circular Parry*
    (*a*) Both fencers on guard in *sixte*, blades engaged.
    (*b*) Defender covered.
    (*c*) Attacker lunges with disengagement.
    (*d*) Defender takes circular parry of *sixte* (clockwise).
Then:
    (*a*) Fencers engaged in *quarte*.
    (*b*) Defender covered.

(c) Attacker lunges with disengagement.

(d) Defender takes circular parry of *quarte* (anti-clockwise).

Both fencers should use fingers as much as possible. Attacker should make his disengagement close to the defender's blade.

4 *The parry against the counter-disengagement.* Only suitable for more advanced fencers!

(a) Both fencers on guard in *quarte*, blades engaged.

(b) Defender *un*covered this time.

(c) Defender changes engagement to *sixte*.

(d) Attacker feints counter-disengagement only – that is, he deceives the change of engagement and straightens his arm, but *does not lunge yet*.

(e) Defender can now choose his parry – any one of *quarte*, circular parry of *sixte*, or *octave*, as attacker lunges.

When you feel confident of the bladework, the exercise can be practised in a continuous action and the speed gradually increased.

In all the above practices, the defender should add a direct riposte once the exercise is going smoothly. The attacker should not try to parry it.

The following points always hold good:

1 The attacker should aim straight for the target, even though he knows he is going to be parried.

2 The defender should keep his knees bent when parrying and riposting.

All the above exercises may be practised by taking a step back while parrying. The rear foot should move instantly.

Counter-attacks – the stop-hit

All the following should be first practised with the stop-hitter remaining in the on-guard position. Later, he may lunge to make his hit. In such cases, it is very important for the attacker to be a good pace outside the normal lunging distance before taking the step forward. Otherwise, a broken blade will be the sad result.

1 Both fencers on guard in *sixte*, absence of blade. Lunging distance.

(a) Attacker steps forward.

(b) Opponent stop-hits by straight thrust.

Plate 5
(*above*) The attack is parried.
(*below*) The riposte.

Plate 6
(*above*) Defence. (*below*) Attack.

The salute: first position (*left*),
second position (*below*).

Plate 7

(*left*) On guard.

(*left*) The left-hander attacks, is parried low (*septime*).
(*below*) The left-hander attacks, is parried low (*octave*).

Plate 8

(*right*) A nine-year-old stylist.

2 Both fencers on guard in *sixte*, blades engaged, lunging distance. Stop-hitter covered.
(*a*) Attacker steps forward, covering in *sixte*.
(*b*) Opponent stop-hits by disengagement.

3 Both fencers on guard in *quarte*, blade engaged, lunging distance. Stop-hitter covered.
(*a*) Attacker steps forward, changing engagement to *sixte*.
(*b*) Opponent stop-hits by counter-disengagement.

4 Same as second exercise, but fencers engaged in *quarte*, and attacker covers in *quarte*.

5 Same as third exercise, but fencers are engaged in *sixte*, and attacker changes to *quarte*. (These last two are slightly more difficult.)

Indirect riposte (by disengagement)
1 Both fencers on guard in sixte, blades engaged, defender covered.

2 Attacker disengages with lunge, defender parries *quarte*.

3 Attacker, still on lunge, bends sword-arm and parries *quarte*, as if expecting a direct riposte.

4 Defender, as soon as he feels the 'pull' on his blade, disengages by dropping his point, lifting it, straightening arm and hitting on opposite side of target.

To make this work, the attacker *must* remember to parry *quarte* on the lunge as soon as his attack has been parried.

The defender must make the disengaging action with a bent arm. His point must be high enough to clear the attacker's arm before straightening his own arm.

When making the riposte by disengagement after a parry of *sixte*, the difficulty of the opponent's arm does not arise. Therefore, this example is quicker, though the attacker must still remember to 'parry', this time in *sixte*.

You may also practise the riposte by disengagement after the circular parries of *quarte* and *sixte*.

Counter-riposte

1 *First counter-riposte*

   (*a*) Both fencers on guard in *sixte*, absence of blade.

   (*b*) Attacker lunges with straight thrust, defender parries *quarte*.

   (*c*) Defender ripostes direct, attacker parries *quarte* on lunge.

   (*d*) Attacker counter-ripostes direct.

Another example:

   (*a*) Both fencers on guard in *quarte*, absence of blade.

   (*b*) Attacker lunges with straight thrust, defender parries *sixte*.

   (*c*) Defender ripostes direct, attacker parries *sixte* on lunge.

   (*d*) Attacker counter-ripostes direct.

Attacker must keep well on the front foot and lean forward when parrying the riposte. His parries, whether *quarte* or *sixte*, should be made with the blade more vertical than usual.

2 *Second counter-riposte*

   (*a*) Both fencers on guard in *sixte*, absence of blade.

   (*b*) Attacker lunges with straight thrust, defender parries *quarte*.

   (*c*) Defender ripostes direct, attacker parries *quarte* on lunge.

   (*d*) Attacker counter-ripostes direct, defender again parries *quarte*.

   (*e*) Defender makes second counter-riposte direct.

It is most important for the success of this exercise, that all offensive actions should be directed at the target, not 'aimed off'.

PREPARATIONS OF ATTACK

1 Step Forward.

   (*a*) Both fencers on guard in *sixte*, absence of blade.

   (*b*) On defender's step back, attacker steps forward.

   (*c*) Attacker lunges with straight thrust.

Combine into one set of continuous actions, but defender must be the first to move.

2 Step Back.

   (*a*) Both fencers on guard in *sixte*, absence of blade. Full lunging distance.

   (*b*) Attacker steps back.

   (*c*) Defender steps forward.

   (*d*) As he does so, attacker lunges with straight thrust.

Combine into one set of continuous actions.

Attacker must make sure his arm is straight before lunging, otherwise a broken blade may result.

Both the above examples can be practised from an engagement in *sixte*, the attacker using the disengagement.

3 *Beat*
 (a) Both fencers on guard in *sixte*, absence of blade.
 (b) Attacker beats into *quarte*, using wrist-finger action described earlier.
 (c) Attacker straightens arm with point threatening target.
 (d) Attacker lunges and hits.
Practise these actions separately at first, as given above. Then:
 (a) Combine the beat with the straightening of the arm.
 (b) Lunge.
Finally, combine all the actions into a beat-straight thrust attack, but be sure to extend the arm before lunging.

4 *Downward Beats*
 (a) Both fencers on guard in *sixte*, absence of blade. Defender's blade should be lower than usual, but pointing straight ahead.
 (b) Attacker bends wrist inwards, beats down on opponent's blade.
 (c) Attacker straightens wrist and arm, lunges and hits.
Practise (b) and (c) separately before attempting complete movement.

5 *Upward Beat*
Practise in the same way. To start with, defender's blade should be slightly higher than usual.

6 *Change-beat*
 (a) Both fencers on guard in *sixte*, blades engaged.
 (b) Attacker makes change-beat.
 (c) Attacker straightens arm.
 (d) Attacker lunges and hits.
Gradually combine above actions in same way as Beat.

7 *Double Beat*
 (a) Both fencers on guard in *sixte*, absence of blade.
 (b) Attacker beats twice in *quarte*, then straightens arm.

(*c*) Attacker lunges and hits.

Practise separately, then:

(*a*) Combine beats and straightening of arm.

(*b*) Lunge.

Finally, combine all actions.

8 *Pressure*

Practise as for the Beat.

9 *Beat with a step forward*

(*a*) Both fencers on guard in *sixte*, absence of blade. Outside lunging distance.

(*b*) Attacker beats as he steps forward, then straightens arm.

(*c*) Attacker lunges with straight thrust.

10 *Change-beat with a step forward*

(*a*) Both fencers engaged in *sixte*.

(*b*) On defender's step back, attacker steps forward with a change-beat, then straightens arm.

(*c*) Attacker lunges with straight thrust.

11 *Double-beat with two steps forward*

(*a*) Both fencers on guard in *sixte*, absence of blade.

(*b*) On defender's step back, attacker steps forward with a beat.

(*c*) On defender's second step back, attacker again steps forward with a beat, then straightens arm.

(*d*) Attacker lunges with straight thrust.

To start with, it may be found helpful to pause after the first step and beat to make sure that balance has been maintained and that the second step and beat will be correctly combined.

12 Further examples for the more advanced:

(*a*) Beat and change-beat, straight thrust.

(*b*) Double change-beat, straight thrust.

Practise these beats first from on-guard position. Then take a step forward with the two beats.

Always remember – straighten the sword-arm after the last beat, but *before* lunging.

Renewals of attack

1 *Remise*

    (*a*) Both fencers on guard in *sixte*, absence of blade.

    (*b*) Attacker makes straight thrust, defender parries *quarte*.

    (*c*) Defender takes his blade away, as if hesitating where to place riposte.

    (*d*) Attacker, on lunge, keeping sword-arm straight, places point on target area which has been opened.

2 *Redoublement*

    (*a*) Both fencers on guard in *quarte*, absence of blade.

    (*b*) Attacker makes straight thrust, defender parries *sixte*, but holds blade and does not riposte.

    (*c*) Attacker, on lunge, redoubles by disengagement, using fingers as much as possible.

3 *Reprise*

    (*a*) Both fencers on guard in *sixte*, absence of blade.

    (*b*) Attacker makes straight thrust, defender steps back with parry of *quarte*, holding blade.

    (*c*) Attacker recovers forward to on guard position, keeping sword-arm straight.

    (*d*) Attacker lunges with disengagement.

It is most important that the attacker should keep contact with his opponent's blade during the recovery forward.

On no account should he start the second attack until *after* he has fully resumed the on-guard position.

Continue this exercise by joining the first attack and the recovery forward together. This makes sure that you are properly balanced for the second attack, which is supposed to be the winner and really aggressive!

Compound attacks

1 *The One-Two*

    (*a*) Fencers on guard in *sixte*, blades engaged.

    (*b*) Attacker feints disengagement attack, defender does nothing for the moment.

    (*c*) When defender parries *quarte*, attacker again feints disengagement attack, avoiding parry.

    (*d*) Attacker lunges and hits, over opponent's sword-arm.

2 *The Doublé*
  (a) Fencers on guard in *sixte*, blades engaged.
  (b) Attacker feints disengagement attack, defender does nothing for the moment.
  (c) When defender makes circular parry of *sixte*, attacker avoids parry by feint of counter-disengagement (anti-clockwise).
  (d) Attacker lunges and hits.

To build up a continuous compound attack first join the two feints together, so avoiding the opponent's parry. (He must play his part by now trying to parry instantly.) Then lunge. Finally, attempt the complete action and *try* to make it 'progressive'.

Remember, straighten the sword-arm on the first feint and do not bend it again when avoiding parry.

Successive parries

1 *Quarte-sixte against the one-two*
  (a) Fencers on guard in *sixte*, blades engaged.
  (b) Defender parries *quarte* to attacker's feint of one-two. (Attacker does both disengaging actions from on-guard.) Both pause before lunge.
  (c) Attacker lunges, defender parries *sixte*.
When the exercise is going well, it can be done without the pause after the first parry.

There are other combinations against this one-two attack which can be successfully used. The second parry may be either the circular parry of *quarte*, or semi-circular *septime*. Try these in the two stages suggested above.

2 *Circular parry of sixte* – simple parry of *quarte* against the *doublé*
  (a) Fencers on guard in *sixte*, blades engaged.
  (b) Defender parries circular *sixte* to attacker's feint of *doublé* (disengage, counter-disengage from on-guard position). Both pause before lunge.
  (c) Attacker lunges, defender parries *quarte*.
Build up a continuous action, as with *quarte-sixte*.

The second parry against this *doublé* may be another circular parry of *sixte* or semi-circular octave. This last method is so useful that we give it in full.

3 *Circular parry of sixte* – semi-circular *octave* against the *doublé*

    (*a*) Fencers on guard in *sixte*, blades engaged.

    (*b*) Defender parries circular *sixte* to attacker's feint of *doublé*. Both pause before lunge.

    (*c*) Attacker lunges, defender parries *octave*.

Build up as before.

In all the above examples, as soon as the parries are being made confidently and with success, a direct riposte should be added. (When the last parry is in *sixte*, a disengagement riposte may be found to be more convenient.)

Throughout, the defender must 'play the game'. That is to say, he must answer the feint with a properly covered parry, as though he were fencing and really thought that he was threatened with a simple attack. If he fails to parry fully, he not only gets less benefit from the exercise, but makes it more difficult for his opponent to avoid the defending blade.

10

THE TACTICAL APPROACH

Sound technique is needed to make a good fencer. Top-class technique is better still, if you can reach such heights. But even the very best technique is not enough on its own. Attack and defence must be applied in different circumstances and varied against different types of fencers. This is what we mean by the 'tactical approach'. A particular attack or riposte which sweeps you to victory against one opponent may be quite useless against the next.

It is not possible to lay down hard-and-fast rules in these matters; to a very great extent, tactical ability only comes with long experience. Nevertheless, this section does indicate certain conditions or situations favourable to the use of each stroke.

Exact instructions on the making and breaking of ground have not been included. This is not because it is unimportant – it is highly important – and one reason for Britain's recent lack of success in international competitions is that the continentals are much better at it than we are. But there are so many different possibilities in footwork that set patterns as such are useless. Practise as much as you can, by yourself and with partners and opponents, constantly altering the speed and length of your steps, so long as you keep your balance and can move into the lunge at any moment. Variety is the key; keep your opponent guessing about the distance.

It is the same with the speed of your blade actions. Vary it. After several attacks or ripostes at moderate speed, another one whipped in like lightning can undo an opponent who has been 'conditioned' into fencing at a more leisurely rate. In the same way, a counter-riposte much faster than the original attack can also spell danger.

On the other hand, it sometimes pay to slow things down. For instance, if your intention is to attack by a counter-disengagement, it is no use making the circular action about ten times faster than your opponent's change. If you do, you will simply catch your blade against his in the very early stages and 'parry yourself' as fencers say. The secret is to regulate your speed so that it is just sufficiently greater than that of your opponent to deceive his blade movements. This regulation of speed or 'cadence' can be a winner in the highest circles.

Change of engagement   You will not be doing this as often as your fathers and grandfathers, because so much fencing takes place nowadays with absence of blade. Just the same, there will be times when the blades are engaged and then the change becomes possible. The change of engagement should be made for a definite purpose. You may feel happier and better protected in *sixte*. Many fencers do.

To change the engagement when stepping forward is very useful. It helps to protect you from a counter-attack and gives your opponent something else to think about. It may also cause him to react with a covering movement or his own change of engagement, giving you the opportunity to attack.

If your opponent prefers fencing with an engagement of blades, there is something to be said for constant quick changes of engagement as a purely defensive measure. It keeps him occupied and prevents him planning his attacks well in advance and making them smoothly. The disadvantage is that it tires the hand.

SIMPLE ATTACKS

Straight thrust   This is none too easy to do successfully when fencing with absence of blade. You may be lucky if your opponent just stands there gaping and doing nothing when you step forward. It also helps if he is slow on the parry. A bit of angulation with your thrust in this case is also a good idea. Your best chance comes when your opponent stupidly advances too close without realising it.

Your straight thrust should be made from an engagement when your opponent lets himself get uncovered. Always be on the watch for this. It happens many times, particularly after a series of steps backwards and forwards. Then a fast, really determined straight thrust right along his blade will bring a satisfying light and buzz from the box.

Disengagement and **cut-over**   The ideal opportunity for a disengagement is when your opponent covers. His blade is then going in the opposite direction to the line where the attack is coming. But this requires a lot of experience and a good sense of blade if it is to be timed right.

A covering action gives the same opportunity for a cut-over. Watch also for the opponent who drops his sword-hand. Many fencers do this, especially when engaged in *quarte*. They then find it difficult to parry *sixte* properly.

But the chief advantage of the cut-over lies in its surprise value so don't use it too often. The opponent tends to 'lose' the blade as it is withdrawn, and becoming flustered and, not knowing quite where the danger threatens, is late with his parry.

Counter-disengagement   It takes a lot of practice. Your best chance is when you have noticed that your opponent is slow and wide when he changes the engagement. If he is ultra-slow, it is sometimes possible to hit him with what is in fact a straight thrust while his blade is still underneath yours.

Low-line attacks   Watch for the fencer who keeps his sword-hand rather exaggeratedly high, or the one who keeps his sword-arm straight, or almost straight. In both cases he is going to find it harder to parry a low attack than if he kept his hand and arm in the orthodox positions. Sometimes you can 'make room' for your attack and take your opponent by surprise by an upward beat followed by a straight thrust low.

At all times, when attacking low, it is very important to drive home the thrust with maximum speed and determination and if it follows a beat, without the slightest suspicion of hesitation or delay. By the very nature of things, the whole of your upper target is left open to a stop-hit.

PARRIES

Simple parries are the easiest and in the early stages of fencing the safest. All the same, it is a good idea to vary your parries if you can. An occasional parry of a different sort unsettles your opponent, and just supposing he is advanced enough to have learned compound attacks, he will be uncertain which one to try.

The **Semi-circular parry** is really a 'must'. Very few fencers use it enough, or do it well enough. It has to be used against low line attacks, instead of the business of pushing right down with hand and blade that we sometimes see, resulting in a 'locked' position from which it is very difficult to riposte. It is also very useful against attacks in the high line, especially clumsy, wide, angled attacks. It collects and gathers them in.

The **circular parry** is less effective against wide, heavy-handed attacks. The wider the opponent's blade, the harder it is for the circular parry to collect it.

For most fencers, the circular parry of *quarte* is the most useful. It has the great advantage of allowing you to make a direct riposte very fast at an open target – no worries about the opponent's sword-arm. All things being equal, there is much to be said for using the circular parry of *quarte* rather than the simple parry of *sixte*. But remember – a circular parry of *quarte* means that you must be in the *quarte* line to begin with!

Parries combined with a step back   Stepping back will give you more time to parry an opponent who is 'crowding' you, or who has stolen inside your distance. Make sure that your rear foot not only moves instantly, but is taken far enough back to give you the space you need.

A full step backwards is essential. Many fencers fail to move the back foot far enough, especially with the parry of *octave*. This can be dangerous against the wide attacks we mentioned earlier, because you are taking your opponent's point across your body. You don't want to do his job for him by pulling it onto your target because you haven't given yourself enough room.

COUNTER-ATTACKS – THE STOP-HIT

The stop-hit is a good servant but a bad master. The automatic stop-hitter will get into all sorts of trouble. There will be endless double hits and practically all of them will be decided against him. Once you see your opponent straightening his arm to attack, get rid of all idea of stop-hitting. You must parry.

Your chance of a stop-hit comes against the fencer who is too lazy to make a really good lunge and therefore is always stepping forward trying to get to close quarters, perhaps even when uncovered or with absence of blade. These are the suckers for a stop-hit by straight-thrust and you will meet very many of them in the early stages of your career.

Even if your opponent protects himself as he should, by a covering action as he steps forward, you can stop-hit by disengagement. This is particularly true if he covers in *sixte* – you don't risk hitting his sword-arm.

If you think you have mastered the counter-disengagement, you can try the stop-hit by this method on the more sophisticated opponent who steps forward with a change of engagement. If you get it right, this can be a winner.

You may hear old fencers talking about 'attacks on the preparation'. These are really only stop-hits with a lunge. The idea is the same. There is the added advantage that the danger area for your opponent is increased.

Don't automatically step back just because your opponent steps forward. Always be on the look-out for the opportunity to stop-hit. You will gain many a hit this way. But as we said earlier, be sensible. Don't let it run away with you.

RIPOSTES

The **direct riposte** from *quarte* is about the fastest thing in fencing. That is why we stressed the value of the circular parry of *quarte* and why in many ways it is better than the simple parry of *sixte*.

From *sixte*, a direct riposte is very difficult, almost impossible, if your opponent keeps his arm straight after you have parried him, as he should do. The direct route to his target is then almost completely blocked.

The **indirect riposte by disengagement** is one of the most valuable strokes. There will come times when, however fast and accurate your direct ripostes from *quarte*, your opponent is parrying them with ease. In many cases a riposte by disengagement will then give you the hit you want. Your opponent will by this time be expecting another direct riposte, so when his attack is parried, he will instinctively bend his arm into the parry of *quarte*. Hold your own parry until you feel the pull of his blade, then disengage, using the fingers as much as you can. All this naturally takes more time than the direct riposte, so your opponent may have started his recovery, and you will have to lunge. Make sure your arm is straight before doing so!

From the parry of *sixte*, as we have already suggested, the riposte will have to be made by disengagement more often than not. If your opponent leaves his arm out straight and high, you can disengage into the low line, slightly bending the knees as you do so.

Ripostes from *octave* can be made in the low line with opposition of blades. They can also be made high. Then, in theory, they are by disengagement. Their value lies in the fact that to protect himself, the opponent must take a semi-circular parry back to the high-line; and few fencers have practised this as much as they should.

After the parry of *septime*, the riposte may go pretty well anywhere. You have practically the entire target to aim at.

COUNTER-RIPOSTES

The **first counter-riposte**   You will not have too many chances to do this nowadays – the modern fencer tends to rely on his attack or riposte, and if these fail, he jumps away with very fast footwork.

Your best chance will come with the very correct opponent who stands his ground to parry and delivers a good, fast, accurate direct riposte. If you are ready for this, you can parry on the lunge and hit him with a direct riposte. This is the first counter-riposte.

The **second counter-riposte**   This is where a disengagement comes into its own.

You have parried the original attack in *quarte* and made a direct riposte which your opponent in his turn has parried. He is good enough to counter-riposte and you are even better – you again parry in *quarte*.

This is where things can become ridiculous when the fencers are beginners. If you both go on exchanging direct counter-ripostes in *quarte*, there will never be any end to it. It is much better to hold your opponent's first counter-riposte and dis-engage when you feel him starting to parry.

We must not be too fixed about these things, but it is not a bad rule to say that the second counter-riposte should almost always be by disengagement. That is, if you ever get that far at all. If you do, you can also use the cut-over, because this gives you the advantage of a change of rhythm.

PREPARATIONS OF ATTACK

The **step forward**   If your opponent steps back for any reason, you will need to step forward to keep your lunging distance.

You may also want to step forward to close the distance and make your attack more dangerous. A sly, gliding step, rather longer than usual, can put your opponent at your mercy without his realising the danger. A straight thrust from close quarters, particularly if angulated, can be deadly. But beware! He may have read the section on stop-hits, so be ready to parry if one comes.

The **step back**   Sometimes your opponent may not respond to one step back. You may have to take two or more to tempt him into coming forward.

If so, shorten your stride on the second and third steps. Your opponent, eager to follow you up, may well misjudge the dis-tance and find himself in the danger area.

The **beat** has several advantages. It displaces your opponent's blade and gives you more 'room' for your attack. It gives him something extra to think about; and what is more, the rules say that he must parry a beat attack before he can begin to think about hitting you.

The **downward** and **upward beat**: look for the fencer who holds his arm and weapon unusually low or high. In both cases even more 'space' can be made for the attack by beating down or up, according to the circumstances. The attacker has still more target area to aim at, and the defender that much further to move to form a successful parry.

The **change beat**: everything said above about the beat applies equally well. The change-beat gives your opponent even more to think about. It is generally more effective when starting from an engagement in *sixte*. Most fencers beat more strongly in *quarte*, and as with any disengaging action, there is no opposing sword-arm to worry about.

The **double beat** comes into its own against the ever-retreating fencer who simply will not stand his ground and parry your attacks. If the distance requires it, you will have to take a step with each beat. Vary their strength. The first one can be quite light, the second much stronger, then whip out the sword-arm and 'explode' with the attack.

We can hardly leave this section without a word on what happens when you are on the receiving end of a beat or change-beat. The safety device is instantly to beat back. This not only breaks up your opponent's plans at the very beginning, but better still, gives you the right to attack if you can see an opening.

If your opponent change-beats, a change-beat in answer is likely to baffle him even more.

As for **pressures**, they are less useful nowadays as there is less chance of a delicate return pressure setting up the possibility of a disengagement.

RENEWED ATTACKS

The *remise* today is too often done incorrectly or at the wrong time. Remember that the rules state clearly that a *remise* is made by replacing the point on target without any further movement of blade or arm, in the same line as that in which the attack was parried. It is also necessary to gain a period of fencing time over any riposte. So you will do well to watch for the fencer who, having parried, lets go of the blade and, for whatever reason, delays his riposte.

Never let yourself get frustrated because that brilliant attack which you really thought was worth a hit is parried with disdainful ease and start trying to ram your blade home by sheer brute force.

The *redoublement* You can try this one if your opponent finishes his parry in *sixte* and holds the blade. The only practicable way of redoubling, in nine cases out of ten, is by disengagement; and from *sixte* you have the open side of the target at your mercy.

The *reprise* is used against the fencer who steps back with his parry but does not riposte. Having lunged with the first attack, you recover to guard forward in the way described in the earlier sections. The second lunge will be made with whatever blade action is most suitable. If your opponent releases the blade, it can be by straight thrust. If he continues to hold the parry, a disengagement or cut-over will be needed.

Sometimes, against a fencer who persists in running away, an extra step or steps may be needed following the recovery to guard forward. If so, you need to make some sort of blade action, such as a beat or change of engagement, as you step forward, to protect yourself and give your opponent something to think about. Otherwise, you may walk onto that long delayed riposte.

Renewals are always faster and more aggressive when planned in advance. This is particularly the case with the *reprise*. You may cut down the first lunge slightly, so long as you remember to aim your point straight at the target; but the second lunge should 'explode' as fast and as deep you can make it.

COMPOUND ATTACK

The one-two, as we know, can only be used to deceive a simple parry. That is the parry most commonly taken against a straight thrust or disengagement. However, it may be tactically wise to feel the way by two or three false attacks – that is, attacks just to check that the simple parry is in fact the one your opponent

generally uses. Then drive home the one-two with real determination, making the first blade action as deep as possible. It is
always an advantage to ensure that the attack finishes on the
open side of the target.

When you are doing your testing attacks, watch out for the
riposte. If your mind is over-occupied with that superb one-two
that is about to come, it is heart-breaking if your opponent just
stretches out his arm and hits you.

A useful variation of the one-two is to feint high – rather higher
than usual – to draw the parry, then drop the blade and hand and
attack low on the same side of the target. But make sure the
sword-arm is kept straight!

Once you are assured that your opponent is going to take a
circular parry, the *doublé* is in some ways more likely to be successful than the one-two. This is because most fencers find it
harder to recover from a circular parry and parry again.

SUCCESSIVE PARRIES

If you are now the defender and engaged in *sixte, quarte-sixte* are
the instinctive parries against a one-two. But as we know, it is
more difficult to riposte direct from *sixte*. Therefore, *quarte*-circu-
lar *quarte*, or *quarte-septime*, offer the better chance of taking over
the offensive with the easier direct riposte to the open side of the
target.

Bearing in mind that the most common compound attack is the
one-two, it is often a good idea to make your first parry circular.
That ruins the attack at the start. If your opponent does go on to
counter-disengage as the second stage in the *doublé*, your second
parry can be the one which finishes in *quarte* – that is, assuming
you are looking for that direct riposte with its deadly speed.

Tactically speaking, combinations of high-low parries, or *vice-
versa*, can be extremely effective and upsetting to the opponent.

THE LEFT-HANDED OPPONENT

These fencers can be very worrying and much practice is needed
against them. The following points may be of some help:

1   The blades are in a different position. Therefore, it is necessary to cover in *sixte* much more fully than against a right-handed
opponent. Otherwise, you will find the annoying fellow sliding
his blade along yours and hitting you with a straight thrust just
inside the right shoulder. You will often find a *quarte* engagement
is better.

2   You will not find it too profitable to attack into the left-hander's *quarte* line. Because of the angle, he can slap his blade
strongly down on top of yours, opening the way for a riposte at
that other danger-area under the sword-arm.

3   Unlike the right-hander, the part of his target nearest you is
his left flank, i.e., his *octave* target. This is one of *his* danger-areas.
How many fencers, right or left-handed, are really confident and
efficient with the low-line parry of *octave*? Straight thrusts and
disengagements from the high line into the left-hander's *octave*
will at least disturb his peace of mind. Supinate the hand – the
blade fixes better when its curve is turned in towards the target.
There is also less risk of its snapping by fouling his sword-arm.

4   Preparations, with or without a step forward may be made by
beats and change-beats from your *quarte* or *sixte* engagement
followed by a disengagement into *octave*.

5   You should be able to score some hits in *octave* against most
left-handers; but if your particular opponent starts to parry confidently, you will have to think about compound attacks, particularly the high-low combinations.

   Alternatively, after a series of attacks in *octave*, suddenly switch
direction and attack for once just where we said he was strong,
high into his *quarte* line – he may not be expecting it and you may
catch him out with this.

6   It is not wise to plan counter-ripostes against a left-hander.
His blade being so near you, it is difficult to parry his riposte at
close quarters in preparation for the counter-riposte.

7   Defence. Everything that has been said so far of course works
the other way round too – your weak point to the left-hander is
also *octave* and as he mostly fences right-handers he probably
knows it only too well. Therefore you must work on your parry of
octave so that you can use it on these occasions with success.

But if you are well covered in *quarte* and he disengages, a strong circular parry of *quarte* leaves any part of his target wide open to the riposte.

FOR THE LEFT-HANDER HIMSELF

Now what about the left-hander facing a fellow left-hander? They may both feel strange and uncertain about what to do, since while there is generally one left-hander in a club for the right-handers to practise with, there are not always two or more. But, of course, the conditions are really just the same as for two right-handers, so any problems should be cleared up by re-reading the sections intended more particularly for them.

COMPETITION ....
Date ....
Pool .... President ....

Order of Bouts	Name	Club	N	1	2	3	4	5	6	7	8	V.	H.R.	H.G.	P.
1–4 2–5 3–6	A. Black		1	▨			5								
5–1 4–2	B. Grey		2		▨			X							
3–1 6–2 5–3	C. White		3			▨									
6–4 1–2	D. Brown		4	3			▨								
3–4 5–6	E. Green		5		X			▨							
2–3 1–6 4–5	A. T. Last		6						▨						

6 Fencers, fifteen bouts

1 /////	3	3
4 ///	1	4
2	6	5
5	2	6
3	5	2
6	3	3
5	6	1
1	4	6
4	1	4
2	2	5

Figure 3: A Typical Pool-Sheet

11

A FEW RULES

There are over seven hundred rules in the Amateur Fencing Association's handbook of *Rules and Regulations*. But don't despair. Many of them are the same at *épée* and sabre as at foil and so are counted three times. Then there are many purely technical ones connected with the electric apparatus which you need not bother with, at any rate for the moment. Again, there are many more dealing with the exact size and weight of the equipment and weapons, which there is no need to learn by heart, as they can always be looked up.

The following list has been kept as short as possible and includes only those rules you need to know when actually fencing.

Pools In most competitions fencers are divided into groups called 'pools'. There are generally six fencers in each pool. The three in each pool who win most bouts are promoted and arranged in further pools, and so on, until a final pool of six is reached. Each fencer is given a number which lasts for each pool he is in. So when you hear the President call your number, you know that your bout is due to start immediately. If your number is the first of the two being called, you take up your position on the President's right hand. If, however, you are a left-hander, you go on his left-hand side in any case. If you and your opponent are both left-handers, the normal rule holds good.

The pool-sheet and **scoring** Figure 3 shows a typical pool-sheet. On top is a large rectangle sub-divided into small squares, each square representing a bout. You will see that the fencers' numbers are placed alongside their names. The numbers are also printed at the head of each vertical column. So for each bout, two squares must be filled in, one for each fencer. In the illustration, Black (number one) has just finished fencing Brown (number four). Black won 5–3. So Black's hits (5) on Brown were placed

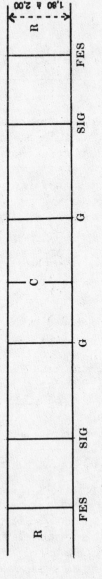

Figure 4: The Regulation Piste for all Three Weapons

C = Centre (line)   G = On guard lines

SIG = Indication to the fencer that he is now 2 metres from the rear limit of the piste

FES = Rear limit (all weapons)   R = Extensions of Piste (run back)

For electric foil and épée the metallic plate must cover the whole length and breadth of the plate including its extensions (run back).

Note: *Piste* is fourteen metres long for all weapons.

beside Black's name, but in column four. In the same way, Brown's hits (3) on Black went under the column number one.

The shaded squares represent the bouts that cannot take place. Black (number one) cannot fight himself, and so on, all the way down.

The bouts always take place in a set order, which need not concern you. The second bout is between numbers two and five, Grey and Green. A light X has been entered in the two squares yet to be filled in for them. Numbers three and six will come after that. See if you can find their two squares. Which will be on the President's right hand?

In the small rectangles below, the hits are filled in as they are scored. As we have said, Number One (Black) scored five hits against Number Four (Brown) in the first bout. The scorer will, in the same way, fill in the hits in the second bout, Number Two (Grey) against Number Five (Green), not forgetting to enter their final scores in the squares above marked X.

The piste (see Figure 4)

1 At the start of a bout and after every proper hit, the fencers must return to their on-guard lines.

2 If no hit has been scored, but the bout has been halted, they re-start where they left off.

3 When the President puts them on guard before and during a bout they must *always* be in the middle of the *piste*, not towards one side. Once the word 'Play' has been given, they can go where they like.

The feet

1 If one foot goes over the sidelines, the bout is halted and you are put on guard at the place you had reached, but in the middle of the *piste*, as explained above.

2 If both feet go over the sidelines, you lose ground. Your opponent is brought forward one metre and you go back to the normal fencing measure.

3 When retreating, notice when your rear foot nears the rear limit line. If you then cross it *with both feet*, a penalty hit is scored against you.

4 You can never score a hit if you are off the *piste*.

5 But you can hit your opponent in the action of his going off the *piste*.

The body
1 You must not 'barge' or shoulder an opponent. If it is done deliberately, you are first warned, then a penalty hit is scored against you.

2 If you turn your back on your opponent, remember it is part of the target and you can still be hit.

3 You must not change ends with your opponent. Once you have gone past him, the bout is stopped and you return to your original places.

The unarmed hand
1 Must not be used to parry your opponent's attack, nor to control your own foil. You receive a warning first; then a penalty hit.

2 Must not even cover a part of your target. The penalty is the same.

The target
1 Ducking and side-stepping are allowed, but if you place an off-target part of the body where an on-target area would normally have been, and are hit, it counts.

2 This is so whether the action was deliberate or not.

3 This rule does not apply when the sword-arm covers the body in the normal on-guard or parrying position, e.g., *quarte*. The sword-arm is a 'natural hazard' and, indeed, gives a certain advantage to the left-hander.

The weapon
1 Must not be used as a throwing weapon.

2 The hand must be on the handle.

3 When thrusting, you must not slip the hand back along the handle to gain extra length.

The hit

1 To score a hit that counts, it is not quite enough to place the point on a proper part of the target. It must 'fix' properly, that is, supposing the swords were sharp in a genuine duel, it would have had to draw blood. With electric weapons, there must be enough pressure to register a hit on the apparatus.

2 A hit which registers off-target does not count, and any further hit from either side will be annulled. The fencers re-start in the place on the *piste* which they had reached.

Number of hits

1 Generally, the first fencer to score five hits wins.

2 The winning number of hits in junior fencing is often four.

Time limit

1 When bouts are for five hits, the time limit is six minutes.

2 After five minutes, the fencers are warned that only one minute is left.

3 When the final minute is up, the bout is over. The fencer who leads in hits wins.

4 If the number of hits is equal, the fencers fight for a deciding hit without limit of time. (Clearly, therefore, if you are in the lead and told there is only one minute to go, it will be a case of safety-first and playing out time.)

5 The same rules apply for four-hit bouts, except that full time is five minutes and the warning is given at four minutes.

The double hit

1 Occurs when both fencers attack each other at once.

2 If they are both hit, only the one whose arm was extended first of all scores.

3 If the President cannot decide who was first, no hit is scored. The fencers are put back on guard where they were and start again.

The stop-hit

1 Must arrive one movement ahead of any attack.

2 Otherwise, if both hit, only the attack counts.

Priority or **right of way** is a difficult subject, but to fence foil properly you must understand it. It doesn't so much mean who was actually first with his hit, but who had the fencing 'right of way'. Think for a moment. It is two hundred years ago, you are fighting for your life in a duel with 'sharps'. Your enemy's sword is held straight out, point right in line with your stomach. Are you really going to tell us that you would gaily throw yourself forward and try to hit him first without first knocking that blade aside?

Of course not. That is why it is exactly the same in fencing. The rules say that if your opponent's blade is held straight out, threatening you, you must control it in some way before you attack. Otherwise, if you do attack and you both hit each other, only the hit against you counts. Not many modern fencers will threaten you with a straight arm in this way, but should it ever happen, remember the rule.

For the same sort of reason, the stop-hit must arrive one period of fencing time ahead of an attack. You are duelling with 'sharps'. So the stop-hit must do what it says – *stop* the opponent and halt him in his tracks before he can hit you. It is no good killing him if, at the same moment, he does the same to you.

It's still the same idea with renewed attacks. They must always arrive ahead of a riposte. Back to our famous duel – your renewal must be one movement ahead of your enemy's riposte, so that it never comes at all. Once again, it's no good finishing him off with a beautifully placed *remise* if in the same instant he drives a yard of steel through your midriff. You want to be the one who survives. So there are reasons behind these rules. They were not made just to be difficult.

12

FREE PLAY

So now you have practised all the strokes described, either with your classmates or perhaps individually with your coach. You can do them! When told to disengage, you disengage. When the order is, parry *quarte* and riposte, it happens. You have made excellent progress, but even though you have had a look at the rules and the section on tactics, you are still only half-way to being a fencer.

The next step is to do everything at the right time in 'free play' (as free fencing with an opponent is called), or in a bout in an official match or competition. This is very much more difficult, and your opponent will of course be doing all he can to stop you putting your intentions into practice, unlike the coach who obligingly gives you the instructions and makes the openings and the distance exactly right.

To begin with, forget all you have ever seen on the films. A real bout is not like a stage fight with endless cuts and parries before the villain is run through. Not that screen duels are to be despised: it takes good fencers to do this sort of thing well, even when it has been rehearsed beforehand, but it is quite impossible in reality.

The beginner must curb his natural impatience. Most fencers in their very early days want to rush at their opponents and keep jabbing away at them. Too often you will be hit yourself while doing so and in any case it does not make for good and enjoyable fencing, or even successful fencing. You may win a few bouts at the lower levels by these methods, but they will not be much use when you progress to something higher. Troublesome though it may seem, you must try to remember what you have been told and you will even have to **think**.

Let us suppose that the coach has, for the first time, paired you off with a partner and told you to 'have a few hits'.

Don't forget to salute your opponent, even if he happens to be your oldest friend. You salute again at the end and shake hands with the unarmed hand, even if, by contrast, he is someone you thoroughly dislike.

In this sort of friendly practice, you don't claim hits; quite the opposite, you freely admit when your opponent has hit you, whether it was on or off-target. Fencers used to say 'A touch', or 'touché.' For some reason this seems to strike people nowadays as highly comical. All you need do, is to raise the unarmed hand as a signal, or point to your target and say 'Yes' or 'A hit'. Remember that an off-target hit cancels a hit on target, (from either side), which follows immediately. If there is real doubt about a hit, it is usual to agree to wash it out and start again.

Be sure that when attacking, you lunge properly and don't just lean or slide forward. It is amazing how successful a good long lunge can be especially against beginners.

Don't just stand in one place. **Move** your feet, use the length of the *piste* and **don't get too close**.

Try to sound out your opponent. If the blades are not engaged, you can try an attack into his open line.

If they are, and he is at all uncovered, you can perhaps hit him by whipping in a straight thrust.

But perhaps all your attacks fail and he comes at you instead. Remember, always riposte after a parry.

Don't worry too much if you keep getting hit. Try to work out why it is, and put things right. If you can't, ask the coach later. The object of these friendly bouts ('assaults' as they are rather surprisingly called) is not so much to win as to practise and improve your strokes.

It is a help if you can set a target – which of you is the first to score, say, three or five hits – even if it is only a mental one for you alone. After that, make a fresh start with another set of hits in mind. This will help to develop the concentration necessary for serious competition fencing.

It is probably better to stop altogether after five, or at most, ten minutes. After that, concentration goes and you start hacking about aimlessly. Nothing is worse for your fencing. It is not enjoyable and the only advantage is the physical exercise – and that you get equally well by jogging or a set of the loathsome press-ups.

The more you fence, the clearer it will become that you have to alter your tactics against different styles of fencer.

1 If he runs at you and 'crowds' you, the answer is the **stop-hit**. But be very sure that his arm was bent or that he had come within distance without trying to attack.

2 Some fencers are always ready to stop-hit. Against them, you must be very wary when closing in for an attack and always be ready to **parry**.

3 Against the fencer who keeps his arm straight and point threatening you all the time, prepare your attacks with a **beat**.

4 Some fencers automatically beat before attacking. **Return the beat and extend the arm**.

5 If your direct ripostes are being parried, **hold the blade and disengage**.

6 What do you do if your opponent parries, but seldom or never ripostes? That's right! You **renew the attack**. If he steps back as well, you recover to guard forward and lunge a second time.

THE FIRST MATCH

This is an account of an imaginary match, but it contains most of the things which a beginner should keep in mind and try to do – and also a good many which he should try to avoid!

You are, of course, on time, complete with the necessary equipment. You tell yourself that you're not nervous, though, of course, you are.

If you are not on first, watch the opening bouts to see what you can learn about the opposition. One of them may be very quick on his feet (watch the distance with him!), another takes a long time to riposte. (You know what to do there!)

There's your number. On to the *piste*, you make the right salutes, first to the President, then to your opponent. The President calls 'Play!' and now it's up to you.

You lunge. 'Halt!' No luck, off target, the hit was on his arm. What now? Another attack? Damn! He's hit me while I was thinking about it. Straight thrust, and I didn't parry wide enough anyway. Get the blade across next time. One-nil.

Now I'll – 'Halt!' Hit again! I pulled my blade over, he disengaged. Two-nil.

Come on, one more hit and you've had it. He's the fastest of their crowd, won't hurt to step back with the parry next time. And don't risk a stop-hit now.

His line's open – click! He's parried, but no riposte, he's going back. Quick, keep the arm out, rear foot and rear arm up, *lunge*. Got him! He wasn't expecting that. Two-one.

Try the low line. Short! And he got me with his stop-hit.

Here he comes again, horribly quickly on his feet. Right! I remembered this time. Blade well over *and* I stepped back. Too far away to riposte. Never mind, still three-one.

Attack low again, but beat first this time. He stop-hits again, but – thank goodness, the President got it right. It was my attack, the beat gave it to me. Three-two.

What's happened? I did something right! He charged in, I stuck my arm out, the blade bent nearly double. A real stop-hit! Super feeling! Three-all.

Beat and attack low again. You *fool*! Thought he never riposted, but he did this time and had all my target to aim at. No more low attacks. Four-three, nasty.

Off we go again. (Parry well across, step back, play safe, he only wants one more!) Parried! Just as I ought. What's this? He's still there, on his lunge. Riposte! Four-all.

'*La Belle*', says the President. (What does that mean?)

His attack, very sudden – skip back – hit on my knee. No joy for him.

'Halt!' That must be it. I've thrown it. Stuck my arm out without thinking and landed on his arm, he hit me fair and square. What's that? 'Together!' did the President say? Nothing either way. What luck, didn't deserve it.

Don't stop-hit now. Too risky. Parry, riposte again, he's parrying these ripostes too well now. What did the coach say? Riposte by disengagement when that happens? Tried it, didn't work, he parried just the same.

What do I – he's uncovered in *sixte*, lunge quick. He's parried me again – get back. 'Halt!' What happened. Against *him*? The *remise*? I kept my arm straight on the way back and he kindly ran onto it.

That's it, then. Don't think I deserved it, I was a bit lucky.

And, of course, you didn't forget to shake hands.

Naturally, it doesn't always end so happily. Sometimes you are going to be white-washed five-nil. Sometimes you are going to lose after taking a comfortable lead, which seems almost worse.

Anyhow, summon up a smile of sorts as you shake hands with your opponent. You probably hate him just then, but looking sulky won't alter the score.

13

THE JURY, JUDGING AND PRESIDING

You will not be asked to preside yet, but in a non-electric match you will be expected to judge. This is a highly important and responsible task and you must know what you are doing.

The President and four judges, two at each end of the *piste*, form a jury. Each pair stands one on either side of the *piste*. The President, as you would expect, is in overall control. The job of the judges is simply to spot hits on the fencer *opposite* to them, *not* for hits on the fencer who has his back to them.

The judges should be about a metre away from the sidelines and the same distance *behind* the fencer at their end. As the fencers move up and down the *piste*, they must do the same, so that they are never too far away from the scene of action.

The moment they see a hit, whether it is on or off target, they must at once raise their hands and the President will halt the fencers. Unless they do this, the President cannot give the order to halt.

It is most important that the fencers themselves should *at once* lower their weapons and step back out of distance, and not stay on the lunge, pushing away at each others' blades and perhaps scoring an extra hit which cannot be allowed, but will confuse everyone.

Judges must be able to tell the difference between a good hit and the 'flat' and '*passé*' hits. The 'flat' hit has no thrust in it, but is simply slapped, or 'laid' on the target from an angle and would not have drawn blood. *Passé* is when the point never arrives at all, but the blade slides along the edge of the target. Neither is a hit of any sort *and should never be signalled, either on or off the target*.

There are four possible replies the judge can give when the President asks for his opinion:

1 *Yes*. (If it was a good hit on target).

Plate 9
Receiving a lesson.

Plate 10
Professor Simmonds' speciality – the double lesson.

Plate 11
(*above*) Young fencers – technique is everything.
(*below*) Group practice – all shapes and sizes.

Plate 12
The real thing – free play!

2 *Yes, but off target*. (If it was a hit on the mask, leg, or arm.)

3 *No*. (If there was no hit anywhere.)

4 *Abstain*. (If you can't say one way or the other, because, perhaps, the position of the fencers blocked your view.)

Each judge has one vote and the President one and a half. This sounds both complicated and mysterious, so let us see what actually happens.

Two judges have spotted a hit and their hands go up. The President calls a halt and asks them if that attack landed properly. Both say 'Yes'! The President agrees. No problem. A clear hit, the fencers return to the on-guard lines and start afresh.

It is not always so simple. You are one of the judges, you think you see a hit and up goes your hand. The President turns to you. 'Yes'! But your co-judge is not quite so sure. He says he will abstain. It is now up to the President. If he agrees with you, well and good, a hit it was. But perhaps he thinks you made a mistake and there was no hit after all. So no hit it is. Why? He has one and a half votes to your one.

One more example. 'A' attacks, but is parried and 'B' ripostes. Up go the hands of both the judges. The attack was made by 'A', so the President has to check with you and your friend that it came to nothing. Luckily, you both say 'No', so the President can hear what the opposite judges have to say about the riposte. They both agree – 'Yes!'

Once more, however, the President thinks they were wrong; perhaps it was really off-target, or missed altogether. All the same, *he must allow that hit*. Why? Two votes to one and a half.

You will be glad to hear that it is the President's duty to add up the votes; you are not required for that. Likewise, it is the President, and he alone, who decides which fencer was in the right when they both hit each other, or whether a stop-hit came before an attack. It is the judges' job to say if they thought the hit in question was, or was not, good; nothing more. Even if they think the President was wrong, they cannot say so.

You must make every effort, therefore, to keep alert and give a clear, prompt answer to the President's questions. Don't just echo what your partner-judge says, if the President should happen to ask him first. He may be older than you, or much higher in the school, or a far more experienced fencer; he may also be a fool, or not paying attention. Don't be afraid to give your own honest opinion.

And don't take refuge in an endless string of 'Abstains'. The judge who does this time after time is either asleep or doesn't know the rules anyway, and is scared to admit it.

FENCING WITH THE ELECTRIC BOX

This makes some difference to the judging. To begin with, fencers using electric foils wear an extra jacket over the ordinary one, but covering the target area only. This second jacket is wired up, through the foil, to the recording box. The box is highly intelligent – more so than a great many fencers – and can tell the difference between a hit on target and a hit off.

Fixed to the box are four electric bulbs, two on either side for each fencer. One of each pair is white, the other coloured. For off-target hits, the white bulb lights up on the side of the fencer who was hit; the coloured one when he receives a hit that was good.

Sometimes both lights on the same side appear at once. This means that the foil hit off-target first, then was replaced on a 'good' target area. Nothing is scored. (An off-target hit cancels anything further.) If it is the other way round (on target, off) only the coloured bulb flashes. A 'good' hit. Don't, please, ask us how this is done.

Therefore, there are no human judges at electric foil. The box tells you exactly who was hit and where, and it cannot lie (at least, very seldom). But the President is still needed. The box, as yet, does not know the rules; and so if the lights go up on both sides, he has to say whose arm was straightened first, or whether the stop-hit was far enough ahead of the attack, and so on.

And there can be no argument about what he says on those matters. His decision is final. Like the football referee, he is right; even when twenty-two players and forty thousand spectators know he was wrong.

A FEW BRAIN-TWISTERS

1 The President calls 'Two and Three on the *piste*'. You

are number three. Which side of the President do you go on?

2 A fencer decides he will have more control if he holds his foil by the *forte*. Is he allowed to do so?

3 'A' is four-nil down after half a minute. In desperation, he decides to fence left-handed to unsettle his opponent. Is this allowed?

4 'A' reaches the rear limit line with his back foot, then takes a step or two forward. Finally, he is driven back across it with both feet. Decision?

5 'A' accidentally steps off the *piste*, then he sees 'B' near the edge with his foil lowered. 'A' reaches out and hits 'B'. Decision?

6 The scores are four-all at five minutes. What should you, as President, do at six minutes?

7 The scores are still nil-nil at five minutes. The fencers are told that one minute is left. 'A' scores almost at once. What happens at six minutes?

8 'A' lunges and hits on target, then instantly renews his attack, this time off target. Decision?

9 The opposite way round to the above. Decision?

10 Both fencers attack together, 'A's hit is off target, 'B's is on. The President gives right of way to 'A'. Decision?

11 'A' attacks, but is parried. He instantly renews his attack, off-target. Meanwhile, 'B' has riposted instantly, on target. Decision?

12 Both fencers attack together. 'A' has 'right of way', but misses altogether. 'B' started too late, but hit. Decision?

13 'A' with 'right of way', lunges and hits off-target. 'B' stop-hits on target. Decision?

14 'A' attacks, 'B' parries and ripostes. 'A', trying to parry *quarte*, is hit on the sword-arm. Should 'B' score?

15 'A' attacks. The first judge says 'Yes', the second 'Yes, but off target.' The President abstains. Decision?

16 'A' attacks. The first judge says 'Yes'. The second says 'No – parried'. The President abstains. But everyone agrees that 'B' hit 'A' with a riposte. Decision?

17 Both fencers attack together. The President gives 'right of way' to 'A'. Both judges say 'No'. The President says 'Yes'. All agree that 'B' hit 'A'. Decision?

18 A hit is 'flat' and off-target. The first judge, however, says 'Yes, it was good.' The other judge abstains. What should you, as President decide?

19 'A' attacks and appears to have been parried, but for some reason both judges and the President all say 'Abstain'. All agree that 'B's riposte was on target. What should the President's decision be?

And lastly, an easy one for luck:-

20 The attacking blade slides along the side of the mask. Both judges signal and say 'off-target'. Were they right?

ANSWERS

1 The left. The fencer called first goes on his right-hand side.

2 The hand must be on the handle.

3 No. Only if he is injured and with the President's permission.

4 Penalty hit.

5 No hit can be scored by a fencer off the *piste*.

6 Time should have been called by the timekeeper when the six minutes were up. Then, if the scores were still level, the fencers must go on until the deciding hit is scored.

7 'Time' is called and whoever is leading then wins. If the scores are again level, they must go on for the decider.

8 A hit.

9 No hit. An off-target hit cancels any further hit from either fencer.

10 No hit. Same reason as above.

11 'B' scores. An instant riposte has 'right of way' over any renewed attack, whether this was off or on target.

12 'B' scores. The 'right of way' only matters if *both* fencers are hit.

13 Off-target. 'A' had the right of attack.

14 No hit. 'A's arm, though covering the target area, was in the normal position.

15 No hit. This is called a 'doubtful' hit. Both judges agree that there was a hit somewhere, but cannot agree where. It is up to the President to decide, but he cannot do so. A 'doubtful' hit is like an off-target hit. It cancels anything further from either side.

16 No hit. 'A' made another 'doubtful' hit. The judges cancelled each other out, the President could not come to the rescue. But the judge who said 'Yes' *might* have been right. If he was, 'B's riposte was not allowable.

17 'B' scores. 'A' may have had 'right of way', but the judges over-ruled the President. (Two votes to one and a half.)

18 No hit. A 'flat' hit, when the point never fixes, is nothing at all, whether on or off target. You therefore out-vote the first judge (one and a half to one) and can consider any riposte, stop-hit, etc., from 'B'.

19 No hit. There is no vote of any sort on 'A's side. Just the same, his attack *might* have been 'good'. If so, 'B's riposte was no use. Another case of 'doubtful'.

20 Wrong. The blade which slides along a fencer, either on or off target, is nothing at all, like the 'flat' hit. The judges should therefore not have raised their hands.

GLOSSARY

Absence of blade	When the foils are not touching.
Aids	The second, third and fourth fingers of the sword-hand.
Beat	A tap against the opponent's blade, a preparation of attack.
Change-beat	A beat on the side of the opponent's blade opposite to where you started.
Change of engagement	To engage the opponent's blade on the side opposite to where you started.
Circular parry	The blade goes round in a circle to collect the attacking blade and bring it back to the position where you started.
Compound attack	An attack with one or more feints.
Compound riposte	A riposte with one or more feints.
Counter-disengagement	An attack with a circular blade action which deceives the opponent's attempt to change the engagement.
Counter-attack	An attack made against an opponent's attack or preparation of attack, for example, the stop-hit.
Counter-riposte	The attacking action following the parry of a riposte, or following the parry of another counter-riposte.
Covered	The blades are engaged, but the opponent cannot hit you in the line in which they are crossed. In other words, he must go over or under your blade and attack the other side of your target.
Cut-over	The attack which goes over your opponent's blade.

Direct attack	The straight-thrust. The position of the blades does not change.
Direct riposte	Like the straight thrust. You do not go over or under your opponent's blade.
Disengagement	The attack which goes under your opponent's blade.
Engagement	When the blades are touching each other.
Feint	A pretence of an attack or riposte, to make the opponent try to parry and then hit him in the part of the target he has left open.
Fencing time	Nothing to do with minutes or seconds, nor the time limit of a bout. It is the time taken for one movement of the blade or body, and is therefore different for each fencer – indeed, it can be different at different times for the same fencer.
Foible	The 'feeble' or thin half of the blade nearest the point.
Forte	The 'strong' or thick half of the blade nearest the handle.
Guard	The saucer-shaped protection for the sword-hand (sometimes called *coquille*).
High lines	*Quarte* and *sixte*.
Indirect attacks	They go over or under the opponent's blade: the cut-over, disengagement and counter-disengagement.
Inside lines	*Quarte* and *septime*.
Jury	The President and the four judges.
La belle	The deciding hit when the scores are equal.
Last fingers	The Aids.
Lines	The positions in which the blade and hand can be held, such as *quarte, sixte, septime, octave*.
Low lines	*Septime* and *octave*.
Manipulators	The thumb and forefinger.

Martingale	A loop on the handle of the non-electric foil.
Measure	The distance between the two fencers; normally, lunging distance.
On guard	The basic position of feet, body and sword-arm, ready to attack or defend.
Orthopaedic grip	A sword-handle shaped to the fingers.
Outside lines	*Sixte* and *octave.*
Parry	To turn aside your opponent's attacking blade, by putting yours in the way.
Phrase	Any series of fencing actions during a bout.
Piste	The long narrow oblong strip on which fencing takes place.
Pistol grip	A type of orthopaedic grip.
Plastron	The protective pad worn over chest and stomach by masters when giving lessons to pupils, who are generally allowed to hit them a great many times.
Pommel	The metal cap on top of the handle.
Preparation of attack	A movement leading up to an attack, e.g., a beat or a step forward. There are others we have not dealt with.
President	The referee in fencing.
Pressure	A preparation of attack, by pressing the blades together.
Principle of defence	Very important! *Forte* against *foible* when parrying.
Priority	When both the fencers hit each other, the President decides which hit stands, according to the rules of fencing.
Pronation	When the sword hand has the knuckles on top and nails underneath.
Recovery or **Return to guard**	Going back to the on-guard position after a lunge.
Redoublement	A renewed attack, by means of a second movement of the blade.
Remise	A renewed attack, by placing the point on target without any other movement of arm or blade.

Reprise	A renewed attack. After the first attack the fencer recovers to guard (generally forwards), then lunges again.
Renewed attacks	Any of the above three. Ripostes and counter-ripostes may also be renewed in the same way.
Right of way	The 'priority' awarded to one fencer when they both hit each other.
Riposte	An attacking action immediately after you have parried.
Semi-circular parry	The point of the weapon moves in a half-circle from high to low-line, or low to high.
Simple attacks	Attacks of one blade action, no feints. The straight thrust, disengagement, cut-over and counter-disengagement.
Stop-hit	A form of counter-attack against your opponent's attack or step forward.
Straight thrust	Same as the direct attack.
Supination	When the sword-hand has the palm and nails uppermost.
Target	The part of the body on which hits count.
Under-plastron	A protective under-garment covering the right flank, shoulder and upper sword-arm. Now compulsory for all weapons.
Uncovered	The blades are engaged, but you can still be hit by a straight thrust.
Warning areas	Coloured areas two metres from the ends of the *piste* to warn fencers they may be in danger of crossing the rear limit.